EATEN ALIVE

EATEN ALIVE

TIM GALATI

atmosphere press

PART 1

1

Sunset gutted the slate clouds red, spilling, and the sun naturally fell for darkness—in the time when everything upstate was gowned in sepia and the northland effigy mushrooms eroded with the wind, when the crabapple leaned and brush wolves ran free, the first few stars would materialize in the east, which is something Embree never pondered until now: the upstate stars. The brush wolves would fight with fishers and run rabbits by scent, eating them alive—nature's vicious, unrelenting ebb and tide. The coyotes' pelts were thickening with the season, she thought, and their muzzles were many times over drowned in blood and viscera. Somehow, someway, she could see in the last arms of sunlight a semblance of a bridge to upstate and independence and the spirits of coyotes and coydogs circling it, mute. Who could know she was an Adenium in bloom? Bless the creator who made the galaxy and the planets and the frothing circle of life whereupon love runs red and dreams walk on.

The Brooklyn evening fell awash with cursed passions natural to Halloween. Streetlights lit and the homeless and pigeons withdrew to their sitting spots. From her fenced-in corner of Stateside Cemetery, Embree heard the urban sea swell street by street with hip-hop bass, grandfather oak leaves rustling alongside her, the clanking of faraway high-track transit rails, and traffic's endless hum and honks. She sat cross-legged by a tombstone: Allison Jean Turcotte, 1972–2014, Beloved Mother. Grass and ragweed smothered the engraving. She left cold and winding down the pathway, careful not to touch the other plots, and looking back she saw the oaks silhouetted against sunset's afterglow. The decrepit caretaker stood at the gate.

"How was your sunset, Ms. Embree?" he asked in his Harlemite voice.

Embree stalled for a moment, tongue-tied. "I couldn't really find a good spot to see it, but it doesn't matter much."

"And how are you?"

"You couldn't tell?" Embree said dimly. "I keep seeing her as she was when she was last alive—too pale, breathing shallowly, but there. I keep expecting that if I dug her up, she'd look the same."

He slouched with his skin ragged, dark, and splotched from poor blood flow, his infantry eyes. He rubbed a grey mustache, his hands so calloused you'd expect dust when he clapped. "How's work?"

"We lost a monster thresher the other day—might've been a New York record. Then the client got pissed at us even though it was his fault and the mood went to hell."

"You wanna hear a story?" he asked.

Embree shrugged.

"When I was a kid I lived in appalacha', the foothills. We lived in a hobbel. My father was a garbage man, and I hunted what I could for the table. Six of us lived there: my uncle, brother, two sisters, mother. I spent day after day in these woods looking for deer, and most years I'd get one. During the rut one day, I kept having flashes, like a vision, of this giant buck standing. I probably seen it five, ten times, like God himself standing before me. The valleys held with a thick fog. The trees were dripping. I figured I was seeing things because I was let down—seeing what I wanted to see. The woods were no better than a desert. I gave up early that morning, hours in, and on the walk home I happened to look up and see this giant deer. All I remember was there was too many points to count and the spread on the antlers was wide, Brooklyn to Chicago," he said, smirking. "I wasn't surprised because I'd been seeing him all morning, but I pulled up the shotgun and my scope was fogged over. He just kept standing there, in the scrub by my hobbel. It couldn't have been. I realized I hadda just point the gun at him and shoot, so that's what I did."

"Did you get him?"

"No. I took a shot at God and came out swingin. We didn't eat any meat that season. Too spensive."

"What does that mean?" Embree asked, her voice picking up just enough.

"Ain't no one answer to it. For the longest time I thought it was truly about being ready and second chances, but no second chances ever came. Looking at you now, it could've meant enjoy something pretty for what it be, however short. Hell, maybe it even meant if I didn't get my act together, I'd miss out on a chance bigger than that deer—like my move to Brooklyn. What the Hell do I know though? Make of it what you will."

"You know a lot Boone...sir."

"It's a true story ya know. Really happened. Just like that. And you know I'm sorry, Ms. Embree," Boone said, pausing. "I've lost all of mine too. You know, everyone has their struggles."

Embree chuckled and cocked her head, grinning. "I love you too much to tell you how I really feel about that line."

"I'm sorry. I didn't mean no offense."

"I know you didn't." The skin around her eyes warmed, and she hugged him.

"You know," Boone said, "it really looks like it wants to rain. I swear it."

Heading home, Embree remembered her father on call with the undertaker and his slurred, misplaced anger the week before he didn't show for the funeral. Still, she could feel a warmth from her boyfriend, Jason, in her whirlwind thoughts. She took the S-train and watched the world outside. Partygoers sat and stood around her and lined the sidewalks below in cliques, a masquerade of more characters and blurred colors than she could hope to hold to memory. She wore shorts, a camisole, and sweater, picking at her nails and crossing her ankles as she sat.

Two days ago, Embree had gone to Cassandra's complex where she had one pigtail died pink and the other blue. They bullshitted while Cassandra raked the goo through brunette locks.

Embree made her way up the craggy, mold-bit, concrete porch steps through an open door and already her father harassed her from across the complex with slurred hollers and senseless requests: beer, dinner, where she's been, where she was going. "He's too far gone to get up," she thought to herself, and in thinking such she felt a strength. The bathroom was littered with mildew, two boxes heaped with junk, and tissue scraps. She had a small corner on the sink for her toiletries and makeup, which she paid for herself. Locking herself in, she started to change, taking off the camisole and sweater and staring through the crack in the mirror crossing diagonally down the offset curves of her breasts and waist. When she was done, she sported an off-white t-shirt trimmed above the hips and cat-clawed around her belly button, laid taut against pale skin and underneath a half red and half blue jacket. She wore a faux gold choker and red and blue short shorts, gold studded belt, and a layer of foundation across her face, decorated with red and blue around the eyes respective to her pigtails.

Embree slipped into the bright Brooklyn night, finding Jason leaning against the outside of her complex, smoking a joint and half-eyeing the streets, boots planted in the only small grass patch for two blocks. He was six-one and built like a linebacker, wearing a brown-gray suede jacket. He was already eighteen, a bit older than her but both high school seniors.

"Happy birthday, lovely," Jason said, laying into her with a hug.

"I love you, but you are a lawless fuck," Embree thought, smiling.

Jason led Embree down the boulevard past its three lifeless trees standing apart like the teeth of a crack addict; past the fenced-in barbed wire block where last week Jason, Embree, and twenty one other residents had looted bare the hurricane stores when the lock was found broken, taking dining chairs, patio umbrellas, water cases, and boxes of chips; past bumper-to-bumper cars tiling the roadsides; and past the graffiti taller than teens could reach, richened over generations, harkening back to calligraphy learned in the third grade. The sidewalk rumbled with chatter and, near and far, certain complexes boomed with bass. They crossed yellow-lit intersections half filled with colorful figures until arriving at Jason's residence two streets down.

Inside the complex worked six others: two stringing silken cobwebs about a combined kitchen and living room, one pouring Nerds and cut fruit and Kool-Aid and vodka into a bin, one stringing donuts from the ceiling, one lining whiskies and tequila along the countertop, and one stashing ice and dozens of beer bottles in the sink. The room was quiet like no man's land days before battle. Embree recognized two — Hailey and Ryan — Jason's roommates.

"How'd you guys get all the booze?" Embree asked, walking in with her bat skidding like a troll's.

"Nice to see you too, Embree," Ryan said.

Two came from the side to introduce themselves to Embree.

"Tim," he said, grinning.

"I'm Nick," said the other, holding out his hand. They shook.

"Hey," Jason said, gesturing at Embree. "We better eat some cake before the party blows up. Free bar's going to attract flies."

"What do you mean?"

"I invited some people on Facebook. Twenty-five confirmed so far. But God knows who they're going to bring. You never know what to expect with these kinds of things."

Days ago, Ryan and Jason had walked the sidewalks for what Ryan called "street wood." They found a chipped slab of plywood, roughly four by six, in a curb heap of rotten sofa cushions, a fat television, and boxes of soiled newspapers. They carried the wood by pinching it under their armpits down three streets and hardly got one sly look. They cleaned it with dish soap and set it up into a beer pong table opposite the kitchen sink by piling the stolen chip boxes and chairs slantways underneath it.

The kitchen and living area consisted of a faux cobweb and Halloween light covered staircase alongside the beer pong table, opposite the sink, which was just a small nook for such an open room. The large bin of jungle juice rested on the counter beside bouquets of liquor bottles. A sofa and miniature round dining table sat toward the front of the room, by the large paned window lined along its shelf with more whiskey and gin. The front door stood beside the window, in front of the staircase. Downstairs, two bedrooms and a bathroom connected to the main room, with one door by the staircase and two in back.

Within the hour, the party blossomed. All but the Halloween strings of lights had been turned off. Pop music boomed. Costumed teens and young adults entered and exited freely through a front door always open, with at least twenty people packed in the main room at any one moment. Cliques stood shoulder to shoulder and their conversations deafened Embree, who played beer pong with Jason as others crowded in to watch.

Tim was already three jungle juice deep by the time the party really started to catch. He never was much of a drinker. He sat, squinting and writing on paper towels along the one small open space of countertop.

"Tim, what are you doing?" asked Ryan.

"I'm writing a story about the party. I'm the only one who'll remember everything. I'm a genius."

Ryan danced like jumping Aborigines to the music, thrashing a trash bag after yet another vodka bottle fell and smashed. "It's not a story. There's like ten words per page. And at least use a notepad. Come with me."

Hours in, most of the floorboards were sticky. Spiderman, Wonder Woman, and Nick had all signed Tim's book, exclaiming in their drunkenness that he was a famous writer. Tim was five jungle juices, three whiskeys, and five beers deep—on the edge of puking and unable to walk straight, so he just sat and continued to write about the party's absurdity: Wonder Woman nagging about chew, Nick spitting from the chew he packed, and then them falling together for a long kiss. The endless alcohol dwindled one kitchen-goer at a time, and a karaoke dance circle fashioned in front of the sofa. Temporary couples formed, played pong, split, drank, reformed, talked, and danced by the hour.

A cloud of ashen hash seeped from the back bedroom, and Embree, Jason, and Tim stumbled through one after the other, finding twelve smokers perched on every corner of furniture, from foldup bed to heater vent to nightstand, passing two joints like clockwork. From the walls Embree could hear the subtle trill of Clicky.

Embree found the downstairs bathroom locked, so over two long minutes she chased upstairs for the other, staggering. In a blur, she saw a mostly open room upstairs with someone sleeping across one couch, a couple making out on another, and a projector casting a movie onto the wall where one man struggled to gouge another's eye out. She stumbled to the third floor, where a hand reached from a bedroom doorway and whisked her away.

Nick was talking about his favorite writers to Tim when he decided to wander, with Tim doing his best to follow and record. He was visiting every door downstairs and upstairs, swinging some open fast.

"You're going to find something awful," Tim said.

"What are you doing?"

"That's the point!" Nick said, and Tim kept just far enough behind.

The oak stairs doubled back toward the third floor, where they found a tight hallway and two bedrooms, one opened and one closed. Nick put his ear up to the closed door and motioned Tim over.

"The fuck is going on in there?" Nick said, trying at the door handle quietly.

The faintest squeals, like a dying rabbit, leached through the doorjamb.

"Think we should get Jason?" Nick said, riddled.

Tim blundered downstairs through the trenches.

"There's some awful squeals coming from your room," Tim said, touching Jason's shoulder.

Jason looked through the crowd and started pointing: "Hailey, Ryan...Jordan, little Steve...Jon...who knows...who cares...where the fuck's Nick and Embree?"

"Well, Nick's up there still. He was with me."

Both wormed their way to the stairs, climbed, and snuck up the second set toward Nick.

"The fuck is going on in there?" Jason said, drowned out by the bass below. He rapped twice on the door and the squeals stopped for a moment then loudened, followed by silence. He took four steps back to the crown of the stairs then charged the door shoulder first, rebounding.

"Ouch, Goddamnit," Jason hissed through his teeth, bracing his shoulder.

Jason charged again, this time leaning further into his steps; the doorframe cracked like the limb of an old, dry grandfather oak kissed by lightning, and the door swung free but sloshed back against his full weight before anyone could get a view. He heard sobbing.

"Shut up, bitch," someone said. "Keep that fucking door closed."

Jason worked at the door with a godlike grip and prying with his elbow and boot as the fingertips from three other hands wrapped back around from the inside.

"Keep everyone downstairs," Jason strained to tell Nick.

Jason squeezed through the door, which slammed shut as Vitoria Scott and Owen Kershner slipped to the floor, scrambling to get up. Rod Bennet stood blurry and bloody before a queen-sized bed, where Embree lay stripped down, a hand on her neck and his devil's prong whipping about and dripping red toward the denim bunched up around his ankles.

Jason squinted, trying to make out the girl sobbing while Rod's friends dove in to grab his arms.

"Go back out the way you came man," Rod said, staring down Jason.

Jason wrestled free, throwing Vitoria through the drywall. Rod hurried to throw free the pants binding his ankles, bending over while raising a switchblade against Jason's lumbering, visceral approach. Vitoria stumbled to her feet and squeezed through the door right behind Owen, slapping Tim aside and barreling down the stairs before exiting with the last few partygoers. Jason and Rod and wailing Embree weighed on the floorboards, their world alone.

2

Embree crashed at Jason's, alone for the first few hours but eventually by his side, stacked on the sofa and bound in his embrace. She didn't sleep and soon morning light bled through the blinds.

"Please, don't leave me," Embree said, quivering.

Embree stirred, chased home, and showered, scrubbing the makeup and clotting blood off; finally, she changed, with her father asleep on the sofa, the TV blaring, and Jason staring him down, waiting. The sidewalks and crossways began to swell with people once again. The streets were dark from the early morning rain. Walking back through the drone of engines and conversation, they heard a kid shout across the street.

"Middleview has a two hour delay!"

Jason checked the school website with his phone, and his throat swelled as he read the news: *Rodney Bennet has passed away. In order to provide counselling services for students, we've issued a two hour delay.*

"This can't find its way back to me, Bree. I'm just starting to get recommendations for school. Even something as small as holding that party—the booze and drugs—can't get out."

Jason touched Embree's arm gently as she zoned out, staring at the overhead transit cars, and she jolted, nodding in time with her lips ajar.

"I'm cold, Jason. I've got shivers."

Jason took off his jacket and set it upon her shoulders.

"Okay, so the party was getting out of hand, and that's

when I kicked everyone out. Rod, Owen, and Vitoria left with the rest of them. Right?"

"What about what Owen and Vitoria say?"

"They'll make some shit up long before they tell."

"Don't leave me today," Embree said, choking up. "I can't go to school like this—with *them*."

"I won't."

Most cliques in the hallways were mumbling about Rod and would be for the remainder of the week. Teachers improvised shorter lessons, trying harder to quiet the kids before every class. In the chaos between classes, Jason found and escorted Embree every time. At the end of fifth period, an announcement boomed over the loudspeakers.

"Jason Newfield to the principal's office, please. Jason Newfield."

Eyes fell upon Jason as he swayed through the halls, guiding Embree by the hand, who only looked down as she shuffled. He arrived at the office ten minutes later, seeing two NYPD officers through the great glass panes. He entered, calm and silent.

"Jason Newfield?"

"Yes."

"The officers have some questions for you," said a secretary.

An officer motioned him down the short hallway to a back conference room. It was beige, carpeted, and smelled of the cedar table at the center.

"Please sit," said an officer. "Are you familiar with Rod Bennet?"

"Not really, but everyone knows," Jason said. "He died yesterday."

"Did you host a party last night?"

"Yes, a Halloween party."

"And was Rod there?"

"Yeah, I think I saw him."

"Was alcohol involved?"

"No."

"Hey, we weren't born yesterday," the other cop added.

"Someone brought booze. They brought hard drugs, too—ketamine. That's why I ended the party. I didn't know the guy and didn't want that shit in my house."

"You're not in trouble," one cop said, writing something on a notepad. "We're just trying to piece Rod's night together. We're not on a witch hunt."

"What time did you kick everyone out?" the other officer asked.

"Around two."

"And what did you do after that?"

"Slept, sir. Dreamt the pigs were coming," he said, cocking his head and rubbing an eye.

"Got it, smartass. Get to class."

That night, cold showers continued to fall. Embree made dinner of macaroni and cheese for herself, her father, and Jason before heading back to Jason's apartment. She stuck to Jason like history to a felon—that is, until Jason spotted far down the lane the NYPD parked outside his apartment.

"You better go home for this," Jason said. "Here, I'll walk you back."

Returning, Jason trudged up the porch steps, swung open the cracked door, and smiled at the detective.

"Remember us?" one cop said, proudly flashing a search warrant. "I'm detective bacon and that's sergeant ham."

They swept over his apartment for four hours: the tight back bedroom, the downstairs and upstairs bathrooms, the kitchen, the upstairs living area, and the second story bedroom, scanning for blood, tearing through drawers and piles, sometimes more than once. Jason sat on the sofa near the entryway with his roommate, Nick, legs crossed, playing with his phone until the police left disappointed.

"Don't get comfortable. We'll be back," one warned, staring down Jason.

The night laid calmly into the streets. Jason watched a rat scurry between alleyways and garbage bins after the crowds of people dissipated. He met Embree at her apartment. She was eating macaroni and cheese again from a folded cardboard Chinese bowl, tucked into her shell and watching TV.

"You want to take a walk?" Jason asked.

Embree stared, rose, and nodded, taking Jason's hand and bringing what was left of the macaroni. The air was quiet and damp. They walked several blocks and found a homeless man wearing several ratty black coats on at once, grease-stained jeans, shoes with holes, and a dirty scowl. He stood on the corner of Grand Boulevard and Cawley Street. She handed him what was left of the macaroni as he stared deathlessly back. Over and over again, the homeless man scooped some into his mouth, then some onto the sidewalk, even after Jason and Embree moved on.

3

A week before Halloween, Embree worked under the table for Paul's charter boat. The sea churned, twisting, parting, and mending in great cerulean heaps and lashing itself ashore. Its whitecaps seemed to them a premonition of more than the forecasted clouds. Embree and Paul were accustomed to the sleeves of cool, salty mist drifting about, and they stood on the concrete landing, their shoes dampened from the rough sea kissing the edge and sloshing over. Paul's face had long been pitted and knotted from squinting, and he took one last drag from his cigarette before flicking it into the sea. He was fifty one. His downeast cruiser seesawed and creaked in the surf, stretching and slackening the mooring ropes. Piped-in fishing poles towered from the cabin, unyielding.

"Maybe we shouldn't go out in these waves," Embree said.

"No way. It's already paid for."

"They're going to get sick."

"That's on them for picking today. We're going. It's the last trip of the season goddamnit."

A minivan pulled into the lot nearest the opposite end of the landing and out tripped three kids and eventually their parents, long-legged metropolitan folk dressed too nicely for the occasion. Paul had run into the father, Dave, twice before in the last year at the marina, where he was gazing over the boats to satisfy his curiosity about casual inshore seafaring. The kids swarmed, weaving circles around one another, squawking and cheering. The parents chased for their hands and walked them down the dock, bent on tiptoeing over surging caps.

"Dave, Joan, how are you?" Paul asked.

"We're great, but the waves are so high," said Joan. "How do you think the fishing will be?"

"It'll be a rough trip, no doubt. But the fishing should be fine as ever. Last week we slaughtered the gator blues. But it can be hit or miss. If we get into them, we'll fill the boat."

Paul lit another cigarette and talked with it hanging from his teeth.

"One thing you have to watch out for is the kids can't touch the fish. Embree will take care of all the touching," Paul said, stepping onto the rocking boat and lending a hand to Joan, the kids, and Dave, drawing them through a gateway along the left stern. "Bluefish will take their fingers off."

Dave nodded. The kids stirred impatiently, fidgeting as Embree strapped them in miniature life vests and afterward tugging any straps they could reach. Embree pictured a man in accounting and a stay-at-home wife—two nautically naïve folk.

Paul slinked into the cabin, started the engine, and pushed hard and fast into the whitecaps, which smacked the hull again and again for each time the boat dipped and rose. The kids swayed and stumbled, holding their parents' hands. Soon, they were miles out, where gales replaced the steady wind and the whitecaps remained. Embree unholstered rod after rod, and reaching into a bin she untangled ten-hook umbrella rigs that were dressed with gaudy colored tubing, and she clipped the rigs to a swivel at the end of each line and lobbed the rigs out and secured the poles in holes along the stern as Paul brought the boat to a steady crawl for trolling.

The kids quieted and one grew expressionless and lost in the eyes, finally puking Rice-A-Roni onto the stern and his dress shoes. Dave held the child by the shoulders. Embree dragged a hose from the starboard wall and used the flow to rake the puke to the stern, and she motioned the family back toward the cabin before opening the door and driving the pale slime overboard. Three rods stood from the stern and began to buckle over, each following the next, as Paul coursed the first gentle U-turn.

"Contact!" Embree said loud enough for all to hear. "Who's first?"

Joan crowded to the back with a kid in hand, and Embree nestled the stout, bowed baitcaster into the kid's arms, which were girdled by his crouching mother's hands. The kid's smile stiffened and he struggled to crank the reel and pump.

"It's so heavy!" said the kid.

"Here, do it like this," Embree said, coaching and taking the second bent rod, leaning back with it, and then whipping it forward while reeling in the slack. She handed the rod off to Dave and the sick child.

Once the first rig neared the stern and the kid and mother were sweating at the brow in the midday air, Embree grabbed a gaff and stuck one of the bluefish in the gill plate, wrenching it over the stern as it thrashed along with two smaller bluefish snared on the same rig. The kid fell to his knees, reaching for the bluefish.

"No!" yelled Embree and Joan, stealing the kid's attention long enough for Embree to lift the umbrella rig. She heaved the wriggling tangle to a cooler alongside the cabin; carefully pried the hooks from their rows of scissor teeth, focusing; and dropped the fish one by one into the ice where they twitched, opening and shutting their jaws as if they were gasping.

Time and again the rods buckled over. The family caught enough over an hour to fill three large coolers, an exhausting effort and too many by Joan's and the kids' figuring. Embree returned the rods to the pipes along the cabin roof and locked a custom cutting board into the rod holders along the stern and laid upon it a bluefish from the cooler, unsheathing a knife from her belt and cutting it behind the gill plate and along the back, peeling and slicing the meat from the ribcage in three quick strokes, parting it from the skin, flipping the fish and repeating, and finally lumping the fillets in a large transparent bag. She took pride in filleting bluefish, striped bass, and fluke faster and neater than anyone else in the marina.

Reaching for another fish, Embree felt her mind fold into a hollow. The front of her brain seemed to itch and her thoughts fogged over. She stalled and massaged her forehead, confused and wobbling still in the surf. Paul steered toward shore for the trip back.

"Paul, I can't do it. I'm lost," Embree said, feeling the anxiety welling up in her chest.

"Again?"

"Yes, sorry."

"Take the wheel then," Paul groaned, throwing his hands in the air.

They swapped spots and Embree laid into the throttle, hurdling over the waves. Paul cut the bluefish slower than Embree but with the same precision and neatness. A kid shrieked and started crying, followed by a shriek from Joan.

"Oh goddamnit," Paul said. "Radio EMS."

The middle kid stood by the cooler with a laceration stretching across his palm, traveling to the bone, and gushing with blood that ran down his forearm in little rivers. Paul entered the cabin and cracked open an old first aid kit and tossed aside the contents until he ran across the gauze, which he used to mummify the sobbing kid's hand.

When they reached shore, Paul had finished bagging their fillets, but Joan wouldn't accept them, holding the kid, flustered and staring back. An ambulance was waiting by the dock, and EMS workers whisked the kid onto a stretcher and into the back and let Joan take the passenger seat. Dave followed in the car with the two other pale-faced children.

"That was a fucking disaster," Paul said.

"I know it."

"You know the gig—three months until season heats back up. Use the time to straighten yourself out."

4

Embree stumbled through eight more school days. She took no notes and sat in class with an undying gaze, stoned by the world's cruelty. She lost seven pounds and walked out on a test. Every night she laid her backbone into Jason's embrace. In moments apart she thought of him and his promise: over the four day weekend, they'd travel upstate to his friend's cabin.

Thursday dragged on until noon, when Jason was called to the office. He left class, crept down to the first floor, and snuck through the side entrance. He walked toward his apartment with his head down, wrapped in a hoodie, hands in his pockets, and from a distance he could see the yellow tape and NYPD skirting the front. He walked to the Hudson, flipped rocks and skipped rocks, palmed crabs and almost considered skipping them too. He thought about how often God thought of him.

That evening Jason worked his way to Embree's apartment, sneaking around the side and through the postern, ducking and turning his phone off. He flipped off her dad, who was sleeping in the lounge chair; he made his way to her room where she sat on the bed's edge, broken and concerned.

"You know, this might be the last I see you for a while," Jason said. "We've got to make the best of it."

They left through the back with Embree's clothes and toiletries and made for the M-train under the cloak of evening traffic and crowded sidewalks. Pigeons smothered the park-bench bread tossers. The alleyways of the subway were dark and the rails girded with great, aged wood beams and a few candy wrappers between struts. They emerged near Atlantic Avenue and already the crowds were starting to die down. Jason found his black '08 Camaro sandwiched bumper to bumper along the curb.

"Kind of lucky, you know?" Jason said. "That there's so few places to park, so I had to park this far away—that we're nowhere near the cops."

"Yeah."

"Never thought I'd say those words," Jason said.

They grabbed the roof and swung down into the front seats. Jason pulled out, teasing the engine into roaring, and zigzagged his way through the avenues until meeting the Manhattan Bridge. They met traffic on the last stretch exiting NYC, and through the stop-and-go crawling he leaned into the passenger seat and kissed Embree's cheek, and she rolled her head onto her shoulder nearest him.

He took the arterial interstates. They stopped in Jersey City against a fierce sunset for gas, where he paid the attendant in cash and watched Embree sleep, collapsed into herself—her small figure. A great divide separated interstate traffic: the northbound and southbound headlights. They wormed their way north over the course of three more hours. He took the gravel backroads of Chenango County through wilderness populated with bobcats, hares, fisher, and wild dogs. A plume of dust followed him in the dark, stones popped from his tires, and half the intersections had no right-of-way signs. The Camaro growled past the few cottages among the pine forests, the apple tree and briar-matted hills, the swamps, and the cold meadows rustling in moonlight glow.

Ahead, a white beam of light flashed back and forth on the side of the road, and Jason slowed and rolled down his window, thinking it was an emergency flagger. The cold November night touched his cheeks.

"What are you doing?" Embree asked, groggy and squinting.

"I'm not sure."

Jason crept to a stop and found a scarred, bearded man roadside with camouflage shorts, a gray t-shirt, and a small backpack waving a flashlight about.

"Thank you so much, man. I've been walking for two hours and nobody's stopped. Can I borrow your phone?"

"What happened?" Jason asked, handing him his Android. "I don't think I get service here either."

"My bike ran out of gas maybe four miles up the road. I thought if I could just make it up the next big hill, I could kick it in neutral and coast to the gas station." He stared at the Android. "Any chance I can get a lift, man?"

"Yeah," Jason said, musing and holding his hand over the pocket where he carried his switchblade. He got out for a moment. "Bree, can you sit in the back for a few minutes—behind me. Push all the bags over."

Embree nodded, got out, slid the driver's seat up, and squeezed into the back. The wandering man took the front passenger seat and started rummaging through his backpack, and Jason slipped his hand deeper into his pocket.

"Thank you, I've gotta find a way to repay you guys. Do you smoke weed?"

"Not much," Jason said. "But maybe it's time we did a little."

The man took four joints from a pill bottle in his backpack and piled them into Jason's cup holder.

"I have PTSD. The veteran's association gave me pills

but they don't cut it, so I got medical marijuana," he said, pausing. "Can we stop by my bike first?"

They pulled up to the bike, and he got out and grabbed his helmet.

"Damn, that's a really nice bike," Jason said.

"Yeah. It's an R1. Had it imported from Hawaii."

"Damn."

"Someday I want a bike," Embree said.

They took the man to the trailer park back along the highway, where he got out and thanked them again, and Embree took her seat back; only then did Jason look at Embree, raise his eyebrows, and chuckle. Jason shot back down the backroads, drifting along corners and spitting up gravel and dust, as Embree breathed heavy through a grin and clutched her seat. They turned onto a long, public dirt road winding through forest bluffs and little moonlit meadows, riding the median berm to one side and to its end, where a yard appeared cradling a two-story cabin that silhouetted against the stars.

Jason reached back for a flashlight, held it out the window, and scanned the cabin, eyeing its burgundy shingles and tin peaks of roofing. An engraving was nailed to the front door: "Poacher's Den." He took her hand and led her around the back, shining light on all the windows and crowns, the mowed yard, stone walls and Virginia creeper, and "Itchy," the outhouse.

"I basically grew up here," he said. "A good family friend owns it. You're safe here."

He unlocked the door and led her in. There were six rooms downstairs: two living areas with nine head mounts of big bucks staring in different directions; posters of women in bikinis; turkey tail fan mounts; kindling, log stacks, and woodstoves; dusty sofas; tables with ashtrays and magazines; a spread black bear skin; a kitchen with a sink draining into open rocky basement and jugs of stream water alongside; two bedrooms with a cabinet holding fuel and dozens of oil lamps, two dressers, and mouse shit strewn over the bedsheets; and finally a narrow, locked-off spiral staircase leading upstairs to a main room and another bedroom.

"This is amazing," Embree said, hugging him tightly.

"Here, look at this. It's all the tickets me and my buddies got."

Embree walked toward a glass display case filled with translucent yellow and white receipts of their wrongdoing. She read a few, smirking:

"Bill Wade. Improper tagging and transport of a deer."

"Jason Newfield. Taking a deer from the wrong wildlife management area."

"Christopher Wade. Baiting deer and hunting without a license."

Jason brought Embree's clothes and the joints inside, and he grabbed oil lamps for the living areas and kitchen, filling them and drawing out the wicks from the burners and lighting each. The lamps smoked lightly and a black soot collected around the glass chimneys' rims. He worked his way upstairs as a bat cried from slits above the rafters, and he came back down with a loaded MP5, complete with extended magazine, shoulder strap, and red dot scope.

"This is what keeps you safe. Nothing will come between me and you."

Embree smirked and shook the dust from a folded blanket, and she laid upon a couch, watching Jason start and stoke fires in the woodstoves. The stoves hissed, spitting a slow heat. He placed the MP5 on the bottom shelf of the gun rack and picked her up newlywed style.

"Jason!" she squealed, laughing.

Jason swung Embree over his shoulder and walked her to a bedroom. With his free hand he opened a tote in the closet, pulling out a sleeping bag and slinging it over the sheets. He laid her into the left gently, then jumped into the right, dragging another unzipped sleeping bag overtop in the thin November air. He hugged her and played with her fading hair until she fell asleep.

"Goodnight, chica..."

5

Embree watched the nightstand's oil lamp cloud with soot. Jason gripped her hard; she couldn't move, and with each moment she felt the stress well up, ashamed that she touched him—or at least so it seemed—while he slept. A half-lit buck head stared down at her with its freakish features, caught in the moment it died. She rolled on her side, trying to hide from what she thought she'd done, from the nonsensical trauma-born nightmares, and finally she snapped free and woke, panting and sweating. There was no deer mount in the room. Five harsh raps came knocking from the door, but she couldn't turn her head to look. She had no control: they would find her and have their way. She woke again while rolling off the edge of the bed, flailing her arms and gasping before piling into the floorboards. Daylight gushed through the blinds, and gunfire in threes and fours wobbled the lamp chimney.

"Jason?" she whispered.

Embree rose, squinting and holding her forehead, stumbling, and she spied Jason shouldering his gun outside the living room window. She rushed out the side door.

"Fuckin thing was right there!" Jason said, pointing at the porch. "Lookin through the kitchen window."

A three-hundred pound black bear laid with a dozen oozing holes in its chest and three in its head. Jason leaned the gun against the picnic table.

"We gotta get rid of this thing," Jason said. "But first, we ain't eatin granola bars this morning. Time for a real breakfast."

With all his strength, Jason pulled at a paw and rolled the beast onto its belly, and he broke out his switchblade, unzipping the skin along its spine and pulling it back to either side.

"Backstraps," he said. "You know—the most tender cut."

Over time Jason carved out two long loins of meat from either side of the bear's backbone, from its chest down to its pelvis.

"I can't believe we got this thing," Jason said, smirking. "I mean, to be fair, Chris told me it's been milling around the cabin some days." He paused. "Hey, shouldn't you be doing the cutting?"

Embree nodded and offered a smirk, still bothered by her layered nightmares as she sat on the picnic table bench. Loose hair fell on the loins, and Jason piled both cuts atop the picnic table after brushing the multicolored leaves off.

"Can you help me drag this thing to the pit?" Jason asked.

Embree took a paw and groaned, leaning her whole body into each pull, dragging the carcass with Jason half a foot at a time through the crispy oak and aspen leaf litter. The fire pit was a mound of ash circled by stone behind the cabin.

"How many times have you done this?" Embree asked, panting.

"Once, with a deer. It's a long story."

Over an hour they built a roaring bonfire atop the bear carcass—heaps of newspaper, kindling, small logs, and finally a blanket of bigger logs from the log stacks on the porch. Jason rinsed off the backstraps with jug water from inside and cut them into inch-thick medallions, and using a pan and fork from the cabinet he seared them rare over blueish coals of the bonfire. Embree watched throughout.

"You gotta cook those more," Embree said. "We'll get trichinosis."

"Honestly and from the bottom of my heart—I don't give a fuck, but okay. Wanna do something different today?" Jason said, looking over his shoulder. "Something fun?"

Embree nodded gently and her face reddened.

"What's wrong, Bree? Come sit next to me."

"You have to let me go, Jason. I'm going to die."

"Life will get better, Bree. Somehow, it will; I know it, and I can feel it."

Embree plopped herself Indian style along the bonfire's edge, leaning her face into his shoulder and beginning to cry.

They ate hot bear steaks at the picnic table with paper plates, plastic forks, and plastic knives. When they went to throw away their garbage, they found the suicide mice that had jumped into the trashcan but couldn't escape. Jason got heartburn but powered through it, smacking his chest.

In time, Jason grabbed clothes from a dresser and Embree's from her suitcase. They passed the run-down barn, winding down along a stone wall and all the yellowing and rusty fall trees barely clinging to their vibrancy, heading deep into the yawning valley behind the cabin. Chanterelles and black trumpets peppered the soggy trail, and the woods changed to a tapestry of oak, hickory, and old pines. At the trail's end, they approached a waterfall where the stream plunged over an eight-foot shale cliff. Wisps of cold, damp air reached out to touch them, and moss, stone, and saplings met the water's edge.

"I just wanted to clean up for later. You can join if you want, but don't feel like you have to."

Jason stripped down to his boxers and smiled at Embree, who backed into a mossy stump and sat. He had a four pack and a little more chest hair on one side than the other. He rinsed and scrubbed his head, chest, and armpits in the shotgun flow of the falls, twisting and squinting as he went.

"Oh my God, that's cold," Jason said, gasping.

That evening, the sunset seeped through the clouds a cold and distant lavender. Jason had stoked the bonfire again and again that afternoon with dry logs, smelling the rot of bear guts, until all that laid was ash-encrusted bone. Embree stayed by his side

"I set something up for us tonight, Bree."

"Just now?"

"A while back. Some friends will be in town. Why, what would you like to do?"

"Oh, I don't know, Jason."

"How about beer and bowling?"

Embree smiled and hugged him, giggling.

"Ok...but I wanna drive," Embree said.

"Anything, babe," Jason said, smirking.

They swung low into the belly of the Camaro in the early starlight and faint glow of the coals. Embree started and revved the purring engine playfully, turning on the high beams and rolling down the windows. She peeled out onto the dirt road leading in, tearing ruts into the lawn, and whisked up and down the hills, threading herself between trees, roadside cliffs, and an ungraded median at fifty.

"We gotta visit their house first, Bree. I have a surprise for you. Left here."

She drifted from one road to another—through the packed-stone, hick Chenango intersections with no traffic signs—until she met the highway.

"Watch out," Jason joked. "NYC driver on your ass!"

"I'm dying to pass him," Embree said, and she laughed in a frenzied way that Jason had never seen from anyone before. He smiled and shrugged.

They were stuck behind a small train of cars on a stretch of narrow highway. The second car of five swerved over the double yellow lines, swerving back before pulling out completely and gradually passing the first.

"Oh my God, they didn't," Embree said, huffing. "Now I gotta!"

Embree floored it, burning out at fifty and passing all five cars through a no pass zone and over a blind hill, including the car that illegally passed the first, and she was laughing hysterically and felt her forearms hot and radiating, beating on the steering wheel with her palms. The parade's front driver whaled on the horn as they sped past on the calico, half-lit highway, but she was laughing, still laughing, until she tilted her head back and breathed off the spell.

"Holy shit, Bree," Jason said, gasping and smooshed into the leather and breathing deep.

They burned back onto the gravel side roads—dark corridors of pine limb archways—with a dust plume following, and they rode until they met a wooded switchback leading to a lit farmhouse on the hill.

"I swear, babe, I must have ADHD," Embree said, parking. "I can't focus when I need to and keep having times where I get really hyper. I can't stand it. I can't go to class. I can't work. I'm a wreck."

"We'll get it figured out when we go back. I promise. Just relax while we're out here. This is our weekend. An old best friend lives here."

Jason knocked at the flaking paint of the front door, and he was met through the cracked door with a stare.

"Jason?!"

"One and only"

"Come in, brother!"

Landon and Camila approached the door, swinging it wide and with Landon coming at Jason for a handshake and hug. Landon was a short stud with huge calves, and Camila was a short, beautiful Mexican-Italian brunette.

"It's been too long, buddy. This is my girl, Embree."

"What have you been up to? What's good in the city?"

"Bartending, bro—under the table at a godforsaken stripper joint. It pays damn good down there, too. So, bowling guys?"

"Yeah," Camila said, turning away. "Let's talk when we get down there. It's fucking cold out here."

They took two cars to the Binghamton bowling alley, Alley Cats, and pulled into the lit lot by the back entrance and inside purchased two games and two pitchers of beer for table three, and all besides Embree changed out their shoes. Embree sat on Jason's lap while Landon and Camila smiled back from across the table.

"So, how's Brooklyn holding up?" Jason asked.

"Good as ever, man," Landon said. "Just drove her the other day."

"What's Brooklyn?" Embree asked.

"You'll see," Jason said. "She's your birthday gift."

They took turns bowling spares as they talked and poured glasses for one another.

"So, Camila, what do you do?" Jason asked.

"I'm finishing up school and actually working right now as an R.N. in training."

"Wait," Embree said. "If I can't focus and get hyper, doesn't that mean I have ADHD?"

"Were you like this you're whole life?" Camila asked.

"Umm...no."

"Then it's probably something else."

"Cam, tell them about the other day," Landon said, winding up for a strike.

"Oh, so, long story short, there was a doctor harassing the nurses—like, sexually—and all these people were coming forward, and I was just standing there like: 'I wanna be sexually harassed!' Like, what's wrong with me?"

Embree immediately popped up and booked for the bathroom.

"What's wrong with Embree?" Camila asked.

"She's been having a rough time lately," Jason said, getting up to follow her. "Life's traumas."

"Shit, that might be part of why she can't focus," Camila said. "I mean, if she has PTSD."

"Yeah, let's drop it please."

Embree came back red-faced, holding her head down and holding Jason's hand. Camila loosened up, embarrassed.

"I'm so sorry, Embree," she said. "Take my turn, please."

"I'm alright. I don't even have the right shoes on."

"You'll be okay," Jason said. "Just don't walk on the

waxed part of the lane."

She stood and threw the fastest gutter ball anyone of them had ever seen. Jason raised his eyebrows.

"Forearms," Embree said, flexing one. "Years of reeling and filleting on the charter."

Just before two in morning, the alley was threatening to close, the pitchers were empty, and crowds around each table were trickling away. They exchanged their shoes at the front desk and around the corner found a claw machine packed with stuffed animals.

"Oh, I'm really good at these," Landon said, breaking out his wallet. "You've got to look for a loose one."

Everyone chuckled and hollered as Landon pulled a teddy lion up from the others, but it slipped from the claw and fell back to its compatriot prison. Several dollars later, he was no closer, and they moved on, finding another claw machine near the exit—this one full of rubber softballs.

"Remind you of something, Landon?" Camila said, smirking.

"What, no way; no way your balls are that big, are they?" Jason asked.

"Just about," Camila said, raising her penciled eyebrows as Landon laughed. "Like a cashew and two baseballs."

"No fucking way. I mean, I have," Jason said, interrupting himself and stopping for the sake of Embree, pausing. "Show me. I'm gonna get you drunk later, and I'm gonna see those things!"

Landon put quarter after quarter in, and on the fifth try a thin-rubber ball came up with the claw, swinging, shining, and falling near enough to the prize chute to catch the lip and fall in. Everyone cheered. Landon held the ball far above his head, and it immediately deflated in his hand.

"Oh my God," Camila said. "That didn't just happen!"

Everyone laughed, swayed, and paced in frustration. Jason took the flat ball and reached up into the prize chute, throwing it back into the heap and rolling a fresh ball out with his fingertips. Embree followed suit, grabbing another ball through the chute. For an hour they threw the balls to one another in the dimly lit parking lot by the front entrance, at times missing and losing and finding the balls in the fenced hedgerow or the building's corner shadows, kicking, smacking, volleying, and bouncing the balls still to one another until they faded once again into adulthood.

At Camila's, Landon led the other three to a gray, tin-roofed garage in the back.

"Taking you guys back to Brooklyn," Landon said, throwing up the door. "What a cute name. Leaving Brooklyn for Brooklyn. She's all yours, buddy."

6

That night, Jason rode back on Brooklyn, his BMW dual-sport motorcycle, and far ahead of him Embree took the Camaro. As she punched it down the dark-cast highway, she laughed in maniacal bursts, ripping at the steering wheel with all her strength and over and over repeating lines of conversation from earlier in the night. She swore she could almost see the light and heat radiating from her forearms.

Embree curled in bed—spooned by Jason and fed by the bear meat, which they wrapped and stored outside in the cold November shadows. She couldn't sleep. An hour after he fell off, she got up and started to pace about, circling room to room and around tables, beds, and nightstands, twirling and giggling. In the living room, from the edge where the ceiling met the wall, a crack began to form, and she stood, head cocked, grinning and watching in ear-ringing silence. As the gap grew, a rotting, tentacled face wormed through and stared down at her, clicking. It warped and flowed and dripped with time. She didn't know what to make of Clicky, and an energy like none she'd known flowed through her, sparking and tingling along her skin.

Embree paced the night away, confused and contented at once. Dust and soot smothered the soles of her feet. An hour before sunrise, she tucked herself back into Jason's embrace and played with his hair, exhausted. She watched the wall melt in the glow of the oil lamp until sunrise soaked the room.

Jason woke around noon, rocking Embree's shoulder

until she fell out of her trance.

"Two options, Bree—old granola from the cupboard or find some fish. What's left of the bear hasta not be fresh by now."

Jason found an ultralight spinning combo, some split shot, and a pack of tiny hooks upstairs, and he flipped cinder blocks outside and gathered a handful of cold worms in a cup. They returned to the falls where he showered, and he handed Embree the pole. She threaded a worm onto the hook and clamped on a small split shot. He pointed in front of the waterfall at the stream's edge of loosely layered shale and the recesses between.

"Cast there, Bree, and give it some slack."

A chunky trout darted out from the cracks, grabbed the worm, and looped back under the shale.

"Wait, give him a second to eat it."

She waited as the line ticked, then set the hook gracefully, and the rod bent over and flexed repeatedly and the drag clicked as the fish circled left and right, finally jumping once and landing with a slap, and it chugged downstream into the riffles before she managed to turn the tired fish to its side and wrest it ashore.

"Oh my God, it's a nice one!" Embree laughed.

They burned time with a few more casts, and then they walked back with their massive small stream brown trout—a twenty inch beauty—and gutted it, coated it with cooking spray, and wrapped it in tinfoil from the cabinet before letting it simmer atop the flat of the roaring woodstove.

They flaked the hot red meat from the wild trout and peeled off the skeleton from the lower fillet, sharing it with one paper plate, one fork, some sea salt, and pepper. The red meat dripped a rich oil.

"Oh man, that's fucking good," Jason muttered, letting the heat vent through his teeth. Embree nodded as he fed her a mouthful.

They finished and Jason whipped the carcass out the door into a patch of forested brush, slapping his hands past each other. Embree sat Indian style on the recliner while he sank into the couch across the table.

"That bike is yours, Bree. Want me to show you the ropes?"

She smiled and hugged him, calm and collected. He mounted the bike and explained everything: the throttle, clutch, lights, brakes, and more. First she circled around the lawn, making a few ruts, but by afternoon she was ripping up and down the long dirt road leading to the cabin. Miles away, dogs barked back at the sputtering engine.

That evening, they found a jigging combo and tackle box upstairs and drove the Camaro to the north end of Whitney Point reservoir. She sat wide-eyed and tingling in the passenger seat, still sleepless. Just down from the Upper Lisle bridge, at the mouth of the upper Otselic, they noticed a fire, a rundown car, and four people standing or sitting on buckets while bait fishing.

"Good news: we made it through W.P., the northeast's tourist trap and trooper hive," Jason said. "Bad news: I think I know these guys. You wanna meet some fuckin losers? Two of them live in that car and have fished most every night for one keeper walleye for twenty years. I used to get hundreds of walleye a year—back when I lived around here, that is. These guys are so sad it's funny; I'll show ya."

They crossed the final bridge and pulled into the dirt lot beside it. The cold wind blew briskly to the north. The sunset was a treasure of cold hues and thick cumulous mountains all reflecting over the waving water. Embree noticed the black shadowing of beard and mustache growing from Jason's jawline, much like the trees against the lilac-blue sky. They got out and slowly approached the losers, with Jason thinking it worthwhile if not for any other reason than to get a rise.

"Dakota, Gary," Jason shouted.

"Who's there?"

"It's Jason. I haven't seen you guys in years."

In the firelight, Jason saw an obese man and woman both in tattered flannel and loose jeans; a younger hunchbacked man standing with his rod and fighting a big fish the most backward, odd way; and beside him the ugliest lady Jason had ever seen, a true sight to see, who was looming over the hunchback man with her scrunched face and witch's nose.

"Holy shit, Jason. Well, this is Eugene and his girlfriend, Candy."

Eugene was reeling relentlessly instead of pumping his rod, making no ground and swearing incessantly. Candy stood next to him, hollering. The fish moved into a snag and only Jason and Embree could see they were shouting and swearing over a lost cause.

"What're you catching?"

"Bullhead," Gary said hoarsely. "But we're trying for walleye. Look what Dakota got here last week." He fumbled with his flip phone then held it out.

"A sturgeon—you got that here on a dead piece of worm?!" Jason said, shocked.

"Wow," Embree added.

"Yeah, it was this long," Gary said, holding out his arms. "We had no idea what it was, so we called the DEC, and a guy came down and ID'd it—told us it's illegal to take and handle them out of the water."

"Well, we're gonna try up the way," Jason said. "Nice seeing you guys."

Embree and Jason followed a trail along the inflowing river to a bend two hundred yards up the way, crossing marsh, thick willows, and downed trees. He gave her the only pole they brought, a stout walleye rod, and to its line he tied an electric-chicken hair jig. She casted over and over, jigging the lure back to her, and every few casts she felt a tap.

"They're stacked here," Embree said. "I can feel them."

"Good, then catch one, Bree."

Embree pulled out a limit of walleye plus some shorts in the dark night with no lights—knots were tied by feel, hooks removed by starlight, and casts made through muscle memory. They could see the fire on the flat in the distance and the arms of light reaching underside the bridge, and they were about to chase back to the car when they heard a deafening explosion. They both jumped and they could hear Gary down the way, laughing.

"The fuck was that," Embree whispered. "That was the loudest fucking thing I've heard in my life."

Jason crouched and guided Embree behind him with his hand, not certain of what happened yet not trusting the losers one iota, especially after some beers. He could hear Gary's and Dakota's voices getting closer until they were just on the other side of the willows, following the river around in a loop. Jason and Embree snuck back to the

Camaro with their three keeper walleye and pole and tackle while Gary and Dakota were looking for them, burning out as they left.

At the cabin, Embree filleted the walleye a minute a piece, despite not having filleted freshwater fish in years.

"Just like a little striper," Embree said.

They ate crisped walleye like royalty under the dying moonlight glinting on webs in the windows.

"What do you think that noise was back there?" Embree asked.

"Maybe Gary shot a gun, like one hell of a pistol?"

"At someone?"

"Hell if I know."

"Was Eugene retarded?"

"I don't know. Something was seriously wrong with him."

They sat side by side on the couch, Embree's head resting on Jason's shoulder, awake as ever. Fires hissed from the two woodstoves, and a light, cold draft wandered from the closed door beside them.

"How about a game?" Embree winked.

"Like what?"

"Truth or dare?"

"Alright, you're on. Hmmm," Jason chuckled. "I dare you to take a fucking shower already."

"In the dark?"

"Yes, I'll protect you if you want. And I won't look."

"Oh boy, okay."

Jason led Embree down the winding path, gun in one hand and flashlight in the other, as snow flurries fell past the last of the rattling canopies. They both wore hoodies and she carried a small heap of clothes and a towel.

At the stream, Jason turned around and crossed his arms after giving her the flashlight. Embree stripped down and tiptoed into the frigid falls.

"Ahhh!" she screeched, laughing.

Embree propped the flashlight on the shale and scrubbed her hair and body for a minute and a half—her lucidity and reservations diving into nonexistence as her thoughts became like lone cards during a dovetail shuffle—before running back toward Jason and jumping naked onto his back, wrapping and locking her arms and legs around his body.

"You're so warm!" Embree said.

"Come on, Bree. Now I'm all wet."

"Shouldn't have dared me then!"

Embree's body numbed fast. She dried off and clothed herself, and they headed back, shivering. Wind howled through the valley as they left.

Jason found a blanket in the closet and laid it across the floor beside the woodstove. They sat side by side and wrapped the edges up over themselves. He played with Embree's moist, tousled hair.

"So," Embree said, "truth or dare?"

"Truth."

"What happened to Rod that night?"

"You sure you want to know?"

"Yes."

"I didn't kill him, Bree."

She raised her eyebrows, still shaking despite the billowing heat.

"Ok, fine then," Embree said, staring and smirking. "Dare: light the joints and kiss me."

They laid and twisted, searching for places to grab,

chained at the chest with Embree on top and breathing deep and slow. Jason reached to the low table and struggled to fetch a joint, smiling, and he pulled a black lighter from his pocket and sparked the joint alight. They took turns toking and kissed between each pass. He wrestled his shirt off and went for her shirt at the waist when she gently grabbed his hands; she felt witch-trial stones on her heart and a chaotic pathos on her soul and mind.

"I just can't. I know it's you, and I love you, but I can't keep my mind off what happened. I'm terrified, and I can't breathe right thinking about it."

"It's more than okay, Bree. I love you, too. How about we unwind tomorrow. I know the perfect spot. You're gonna love it."

"I don't want this to end, babe. Let's never go back."

They made out for an hour until they laid back, side by side, exhausted, and they fell asleep late in the night, their arms tangled and finally warm.

Embree was the first to wake to the sound of Clicky louder and louder haunting her nightmare; she dreamt again that she lost control and took advantage of Jason, and she jumped from the floor in a panting fury. Daybreak wept through the east-facing windows.

"Sleep, Bree," Jason said groggily.

Embree couldn't. Two hours left her more awake and alert than ever. She paced in circles about the rooms and for a moment swore she saw Clicky's rotting face jutting from a fissure in the wall.

By late afternoon, Embree had fallen in and out of a confused and frenzied mood several times, and Jason woke right after she fell back in.

"Babe, let's go for a ride! I want to see the beautiful place," Embree said, grabbing him by the shoulder.

"In the Camaro?"

"No, on the bike!"

"It's not really a two person bike, Bree."

Embree scowled.

"Ok," Jason said, "but I should drive. We were almost there last night. It's off a dirt road in Chenango Forks. This time of year it's full of...well, I'll let you see for yourself."

They boarded the bike in the late afternoon, Embree hugging and smooshing herself into Jason's back, clothed in jeans and a hoodie, and laughing madly before they took off.

"What's gotten into you, Bree? You okay?"

Embree didn't answer; rather, she kept laughing on and off. Jason started the engine and revved it, creeping toward the dirt road and turning hard over old ruts before quickening. She tucked her legs up with nowhere to rest her feet, barely fitting her ass on the seat's edge.

"Detour first. I gotta know what that was last night," Jason said. "Let's stop by Point and check it out."

Gary and Dakota were already in their usual spot fishing by the parking lot, and Jason and Embree pulled up alongside them, keeping the engine running, with Jason shielding Embree from the losers with his body.

"What the fuck happened over here last night?" Jason asked Gary. Dakota was on the phone.

"Oh, I threw a can of bug spray in the fire," Gary said.

Jason killed the engine and laughed hard.

"Eugene," Dakota said over the phone, "why don't you tell Jason how you were so scared last night from the blast that you pissed your pants."

All they could make out was Eugene's flood of cussing sputtering from the phone. They left, en route to the beautiful place.

It began to sprinkle as they sped down the back roads. Nearing the highway, Embree began to shout.

"Faster, open'r up!"

Jason got the bike up to forty five and began to lean into a turn, gunning it and cutting the turn sharp over the gravel shoulder, when the tires squealed and started to slip out, and the bike collapsed, sliding and grinding and sparking ahead of them both, and they skidded on their backs down the next wet straightaway until the clothes burned from their backs and asses, spinning with their limbs out until he could sit up and grab Embree and wrap his body and arms around her, his treasure, before skidding backwards neck-first into a guardrail, and she slipped from his grip as the guardrail gonged like a cathedral bell, ricocheting off his body and tumbling and sliding to a stop. She rose and stumbled, bending her head back and laughing wildly, cherry-red along the backs of her arms, shoulders, and thighs, and she skipped and stumbled her way to Jason, staggering in circles beside him.

"I'm so sorry, Jason—they're going to think you hurt me and they're going to put you down. I'm so sorry."

Embree kept repeating herself and pacing, confused and beaming with energy and dripping blood at her elbows. Whenever she looked up, a head-hung demon was standing still off to the side, first rotting at the skin and afterwards not.

"Fuck off, Vinny," she shouted, charging him before he disappeared.

A bystander parked with his flashers on and called EMS, who arrived and strapped Embree to a stretcher.

"You're not putting him down!" Embree shouted, laughing the next moment.

"She's delusional," one EMT said to another, loading the stretcher. "Clearly having an episode."

One looked to the side. "What a fuckin mess."

"Yup, that's why you wear a helmet."

PART 2

7

As a child, Embree's hair shined a beautiful brunette-black, and the rare times she smiled revealed her little dimples. Before her move to Brooklyn during middle school, she was a single child in a volatile one-story home in Gloversville, a town as dystopic as her parents were dysfunctional. She watched women fight in the streets, pulling at each other's hair and kicking. At the diner, scumbags would never tip. The lanes of houses stood decrepit like sets of gap teeth, and year by year, more people sold their houses and left than moved in. The town was a tick on a dying carcass; the town was rotting away.

Embree's mother had been on dialysis for years—some people are fortunate and others fall through the cracks. The dialysis boxes towered against the living room wall, straight to the ceiling, in neat stacks surrounding an old television stand and a recliner ripping at the seams. This was her favorite place to rest.

The kitchen was a heartache of dirty pots, pans, and silverware strewn about the countertop; fruit flies hatching from the drainage pipe, schooling over loose sugar grains near the coffee, and together waltzing; maggots in the sink bin, all inching along where old scraps of food lay; and clutter everywhere, from overflowing garbage bins to boxes of knickknacks to unused foldup chairs to a moldy fridge.

One stormy day, Embree was age ten and her parents revved against each other until they were hollering—both upstairs. She heard her father close a door so hard that the doorframe cracked. They followed each other to the kitchen when Embree interjected.

"Can you two, like, fuck off? I can't hear the TV."

Embree's father walked over and slapped her across the face, inspiring her mother to scream back.

"Don't you dare do that to her!"

"If you talk to me like that again, there won't be a fucking TV."

Embree squinted back and ran out the paint-chipped front door, gathering a flashlight and five gallon bucket from the sunporch as she went. The sky pissed on her in cold, uncomfortable sheets, blowing crossways, first smothering her hair and shoulders, then in minutes her whole body, weighing down her jeans and t-shirt. A middle-aged man limped in small steps along the curb, cane in hand and wearing a trash bag, sporting a determined scowl as if he had somewhere to go well beyond the maw of the farthest thunderhead. She worked her way past the man by scuffing down the street's median.

Embree passed a mile or more beyond the neglected yards and rusty curb-parked pickup trucks, making her way to a park where one swing chain was broken and the tennis court edges and baseball field were wild and choked with purslane and bull thistle. A concession stand stood graffitied by the baseball pit. Soaked, she loosened up knowing she couldn't get any wetter, softening her stare. She got on her knees at the park's center, pray-posing in curtains of rain, her bucket beside her, and she began to sift through the hay, dandelions, and broadleaf plantain. One by one, she plucked and bucketed the evening nightcrawlers peeking and creeping from their flooded holes, her arms fast and hovering like that of a praying mantis. They were everywhere. She took breaks from picking, leaning back with her eyes closed to the great dark sheet of clouds, letting the cramps work out of her forearms. She inched forward, one knee at a time, dragging the tops of her toes through the little jungle as they reached out from her sandals.

Embree had crawled a hundred yards when she met the blacktop pathway looping through the edge of the park, and there on the path she found a migration of worms—too many to count. She dragged her bucket along—grating by the bottom, half full, and bending by its handle—and continued to fill her bucket, flashlight in hand, the great sheet of gray above reddening to the west and blackening, until the handle sunk painfully into her palms.

Exhausted, Embree stumbled back to the main road, sweating in the cooling nighttime showers, and thirty feet at a time she dragged the bucket, lumbering backwards and looking over her shoulder. She nearly wretched from the hours of wafting worm slime.

By the time Embree arrived on Hober Street, her palms were bruised; she was dazed and drowned in loneliness and determined in her want for freedom. She dragged her bucket to the townhouse where Hank's family lived, continued into his backyard, and rang the doorbell of what struck her as a garage. Light suddenly escaped from the doorjamb.

"Come in!" Hank shouted.

Inside, the walls were plastered with racks of bagged jigs and jig heads, stickbaits, floats, hooks, crankbaits, fading photos of catches, fish mounts, multicolored buck tails, leaders, and so much more that she was working to recognize. A woodstove, a computer, and a recliner with a blanket laid beyond the jutting glass countertop, which displayed antique reels by the register.

"What's happenin' little girl?"

"I want to make a deal," Embree said, two-handed dragging her bucket up to Hank.

"Oh, you got a lot of worms there, sweetheart."

"I know you'll give me a deal," Embree said, twinkling and holding up her palms and head-to-toe soppy.

"You dragged that bucket all the way here?" Hank paused. "Dear God. How's twenty dollars sound?"

"Is that what the Asians get?"

"Oh, I've told you that before?" Hank said, lowering his voice. "Well, I'll cut you a deal better than I do for them. They only get a quarter. I'll give you half. How's that sound?"

Embree nodded, smiling and twinkling; cuteness her only recourse. They walked into a side room, which was well insulated with the air conditioning blasting. Deep tubs held clouds of bait: minnows, shiners, suckers, and more, and a net, bucket, and scale hung from the ceiling. Hank poured her worms across an acrylic countertop, spreading them with his fingertips and sliding them across in fives before slipping twenty five off the edge and into a styrofoam cup. He made fast work of them, filling dozens of cups and setting them aside to be packed with dirt later. He rinsed his hands and waddled back to the register.

"Shut that door, please."

Hank handed her a small wad of twenties.

"Thank you, Hank."

"Rule one: count your money. Rule two: never trust a fisherman." Hank reached into the register and handed over ten dollars more. "That's half—seventy clams."

Embree turned for the door.

"You know," Hank said, "you best be careful with them nigger gangs out there."

"Huh?"

"Don't flash that money in the streets."

Embree pocketed the money, leaving with her empty bucket. Thunder roared across the mountains. Another three miles brought her to Walmart, where her soppy shoes squeaked with every step—and most everyone looked at her as she passed. Toward the back, she found a boxed sixty dollar two-person tent, loaded it into her bucket, and made for the cashier, grabbing the biggest pack of M&Ms they had along the way. She hoisted the bucket onto the conveyer and slapped the wad of money next to it, smiling. The cashier glared back through her.

"Paper or plastic?"

"Bucket, please."

"Have a good one," the cashier muttered, letting change and receipt slip into the bucket.

Five wandering, winding miles—wet trails in people's yards from the dragging bucket, trails that wouldn't live long in such heavy rain—led Embree back home. She strained to connect tent poles and slide them through the material moorings of the tent as rain turned to small hail and again the thunder reigned. She barged back into the house.

"Where the fuck have you been?" the father asked.

Embree flipped him off, grinning and swinging her hips, and then climbed upstairs to her room and grabbed a pillow, blanket, IPod, fresh clothes, and several books. She escaped back outside and packed her tent like a rat, piling soaked clothes beside a crumpled blanket and pillow, the rain and hail still pelting the tent and the wind threatening to tear it from its anchor pins. She stayed in her tent anytime her parents fought that summer, reading the few freshwater fishing and survival books her mother had got her for her past birthday and missing the few times they fished together long past—before illness beset them both. Her mom brought out food regularly, trying her best to respect Embree's distance while taking special care of her.

8

Struggle—what everything in Embree's life amounted to, or so she thought—struggle and control. She thrashed against leather four-point restraints, an eruption of disorganized thought, anger, elated confusion, and crying. She felt held by a tightness like she hadn't since the party, a tightness which pushed her to shrieking and laughing as the metal gurney scissored open, expanding and rattling when the EMTs brought the gurney from ambulance to sidewalk, through cold sleet, and past the automatic sliding hospital doors.

"Jason!" Embree spat, wide-eyed. "I don't want to be touched!"

They carted Embree around the attendant's desk past staring nurses to a series of ten curtain cubicles, backing her into the final one. She heard the ailing, aching, and talking of her people in the sections down the line. A nurse came by in the first few minutes.

"Honey, can I take a look at you?"

She hissed back, but the nurse insisted, lifting her red-burned arms and calves as well as her head. Half an hour passed before the doctor approached her.

"Where's Jason," Embree laughed.

"Embree, that is your name, right? Mild whiplash, road burn—from what I heard, you made out way better than you should have. Except your mind—you seem to be having some kind of episode, manic or psychotic or both, and we can't treat that here. We'll move you upstairs."

The doctor whispered to two nurses, and Embree went back to flexing and trying to rip her arms from the leathers. The ambulance crew had set up an IV in her forearm, and through that the doctor injected a slug of lorazepam, and she faded quickly. They wrapped her road-burned areas in bandages, with blood seeping through along her calves, and they worked to move her out and upstairs via the stretcher. In the elevator, she started to doze off, entering some delirious state where she thought she was talking to Jason beside the nurses.

"Jason my neck hurts. We forgot to give the mail man his peanut butter," she mumbled.

Embree was out cold by the time she arrived at her room upstairs, in the higher level psychiatric ward. She remained strapped in. Every so often a nurse would peer through the door's reinforced window into the empty off-white room.

Later that night, when Embree started to wake, she found a doctor at her side, and it pained her to twist her neck and stare back. She felt a cold compress cradling her neck, and she found the bandages wrapping along stretches of her legs and arms.

"What happened? Where the fuck am I?" Embree said. "Where's Jason?"

"You were in an accident along the highway. The guard rail, well, to put it frankly, the accident—well, he isn't with us anymore. I'm so sorry."

Embree's face and fists flexed taut, and she huffed through her nostrils before beginning to cry. The doctor waited with her, a hand on her bandaged arm, until her crying broke into spurts.

"Tell me, in the past week have you been irritable or aggressive, overjoyed or hyper, sad or apathetic?"

"Umm, I guess so."

"Which?"

"All of them. I thought I had ADHD," she said, sniffling. "I can't focus in school or anywhere really."

"When did this start?"

"A couple months ago, and sometimes, yes, I'd get really hyper and overwhelmed with energy."

"How was your sleep?"

"All over the place. I slept in and missed classes some days, and other days I was awake for days—energy like nothing I've ever known, like I said."

"And did you feel anything else in the past?"

"There were a couple stretches where I felt depressed, one worse than the other. I tried taking supplements and they sorta helped I think. I figured I had a problem, but I was afraid of this place—here."

"What is wrong with here?"

"I wanted control and freedom, the opposite of psych wards."

"That's the old days. Now we're a psychiatric hospital. We operate almost the same as a regular hospital, and we care about all of our patients. The biggest reason you're strapped to the gurney is to protect you from yourself."

Embree noticed the good doctor's white button-down coat. Vinny appeared alongside her, dripping.

"Wait, who are you again?"

"I'm Dr. Halsey. What are you staring at?"

"Vinny."

"Who's Vinny?"

"He's an asshole."

"That doesn't really answer my question."

"Good."

They paused.

"Embree, I'm on your side here. Do you want to get better?

"I don't fuckin care right now," Embree cried. "I want Jason. I want out of these things."

"If I let you out, will you cooperate?"

"Sure."

The doctor left and returned with a nurse and a cup.

"Are you familiar with bipolar disorder, Embree?"

"Not really—why, you think that's me?" she choked.

"Perhaps later would be a better time, no?"

Embree nodded.

"Would you like to try this before I go?"

Embree nodded again—her risk taking once again unrestrained—and a final tear fell, meandering down her cheek. The nurse and doctor unleashed her wrists and ankles, handing her the cups as she raised, wobbling, and she tipped forward, zapped by the lorazepam, taking and swallowing the pill and water and falling back.

"Thank you," Embree muttered as they left.

9

Embree woke to the plainclothes doctor looming over her with a professional nametag and a clipboard while saying her name.

"Embree, your father's on the line."

Embree rolled from the stretcher and felt the blood rush to her extremities, standing. They walked to the landline in the hallway outside the room where a nurse handed her the phone.

"Dad?"

"I can't believe you. Don't bother coming home."

A click shot through the phone before she could answer, but she tried anyway.

"How's it feel to kill another one, dad?"

Embree handed the doctor the phone, brushing the hair from her face.

"Can I take a shower here?"

"Yes, yes of course. Follow me."

Dr. Halsey escorted Embree with a hand on her shoulder down the hall to the humble restroom barren of grooming tools and other amenities where she slipped inside, and the nurse waited for her just outside the closed door. Inside she removed her bandages, stretching in view of a mirror to see the brandished backs of her arms and legs and rubbing them. She stretched her legs one at a time like a cat across the sink basin, and she stripped down, throwing the clothes in a basket. In the shower, she scrubbed her body and the few pieces of grit collected still on her feet with generic soaps, remembering the feel and sound of the gravel during the crash but nothing more of it. Stepping out, she sighed: the comfort of her toes on the mat, the towel raking her scalp and breasts and limbs, the coolness wrapping around her and, in that, the taste of captive freedom. To the left, she chose from a shelved cabinet packed with t-shirts, jeans, underwear, and loose socks—everything else fitting tight. The nurse guided her back to her room, and the doctor entered shortly thereafter.

"Embree, have you heard of bipolar disorder?"

"Yes, you mentioned it yesterday."

"Funny, I mean do you know anything about it?"

"Nope."

The doctor paged through a copy of the DSM 5.

"You're having mood swings, right?"

"I guess," she said, nodding.

"Well, just hear me out. Mood swings range from depression to mania. Mania includes difficulty concentrating; insomnia; restlessness; irritability; hyperactivity; hypersexuality; impulsivity; rapid thoughts; frenzied speaking; and in serious cases of bipolar one, delusions, hallucinations, and paranoia. Depression usually includes lowered energy, motivation, concentration, and interest in activities, as well as too much or too little sleep, changes in appetite and weight, and thoughts of suicide."

"Oh my god," Embree thought, letting her lips part.

"You don't need to have all the symptoms to be diagnosed, but I'm guessing some of those ring true for you?"

Embree nodded.

"Are you finding this interesting? Do you want to hear more?"

Embree nodded slowly.

"There are different categories of bipolar. Bipolar one includes psychosis or mania severe enough to require hospitalization, and it usually includes depression but doesn't have to. Bipolar two is like one but includes no true mania, only depression and a lesser version of mania known as hypomania, so it includes no psychosis. Then bipolar three, or cyclomania, includes periods of mild depression and hypomania. And bipolar four, or BPNOS, is where someone falls if they show signs of bipolar but their symptoms are nontraditional."

Embree took a deep breath amongst dead silence. She was starting to cry again.

"Embree, are you seeing things or hearing voices?"

"Yes," Embree sniffled. "Vinny and Clicky. Usually, Vinny drips and Clicky clicks."

"Do you want the good news, bad news, or worst news?"

Embree nodded.

"Which?"

"All of it."

"The good is that mood disorders are treatable and many people go on to live productive, happy lives. The bad news is hypomania can actually be a productive state for bipolar people, and because of that bipolar people are the number one group that defects from their medication. The other bad news is that finding the right medication regiment can be a frustrating, long, even painful process. The worst news is that a petition was filed with no certificate, so we can't legally hold you here more than forty-eight hours, unless of course you'd like to admit yourself as a voluntary patient. We can consult you, however, on how to get help when you leave."

The doctor found her pen and clipboard, flipped to the back, and began to scribble. "You should see a psychiatrist regularly. You can choose whoever you like, but I'd recommend Dr. Noham. Do you want her number?"

Embree nodded, weeping now over memories of Jason. The doctor flipped back and forth through her notes.

"I gave you a low dose of lithium yesterday to start. You'll likely need more than that, including an antipsychotic."

Embree stared to the side, crying.

"Do you want to get better, Embree?"

"Of course."

"Then I recommend strongly that you follow through with this," the doctor said, handing her the sheet. "How about some breakfast and a new room? Now that you're more stable, I can take you to the first floor. You can interact with other patients, watch television, have your phone and wallet back, and have your own bed and restroom."

Embree's teary eyes lit up.

Together they descended by elevator into a catacomb of her people: the schizophrenics, the personality disorderlies, the mood abjects. Walls fused to tiling off-white all around in the tunnel filled with shouting, crying, a strapped patient, strolling unstrapped patients, patients lost in the eyes, nurses, and themselves.

"I don't want to be here! I've been here eleven years! Nothing works!" one shouted.

They walked to her new unadorned room, scanning it over, and then strolled to a lounge with sofas where two patients were watching medical documentaries—psychiatric week specials.

"Are you going to be okay down here, Embree?"

"I guess, yes."

"I'll be around if you need me, and I'll send a nurse for food."

Embree ordered buttered toast and eggs and wandered to a window and cried, eyeing the urban squares below choked with drivers and dog walkers and bench sitters and parkway trees and all of their simplicity and freedom. Air blasted through the ceiling vents. A hand touched her shoulder and she jumped and shrieked.

"I don't want to be touched!"

"Honey, here's your food and phone. Are you doing okay?"

Embree nodded unconsciously.

That evening, in the hallway, Embree met an elderly woman dressed in a patient's gown while wheeling through the halls aimlessly. From the nurse's hub, her doctor smiled at her, so she decided to follow the old woman to the lounge.

"What're you here for?" Embree asked.

"Schizophrenia."

"How's that work?"

"They tell me to do bad things," the old woman said. "I like you. I think this is the end of my world!" she said, wheeling away.

Embree moved to her room for most of the next morning after a stocky, autistic man hit on her several times during breakfast.

By afternoon, Embree ended up making a call to Camila, who picked up the phone immediately.

"Embree? What's up?"

"Jason and I crashed," Embree wept. "He died. I have nobody to help me."

"Oh my God, no!"

"I'm lost."

Embree welled up in the silence.

"We don't have much but we'll take you in, honey."

"Thank you. I'm at the Binghamton hospital for crazies. I get out soon."

On the sidewalk, beside the rustling black locust plots with their late brown leaves, stood Embree, waiting. She reached toward a cigarette disposal stand, folding the notes of the psychiatrist referral into a thin stalk and shoving it down the gap.

"Of course," she said.

10

The lights were off and Embree tried at the light switch, but the bulb was out and nothing would work and a panic settled in as she wormed across the dark room through the doorway to the dim-lit next. She kept working her way across the flat until she visited all the rooms, searching for light, unsettled and tousled at the hair and holding herself for protection from the monsters within that she knew were ready to pounce on and restrain and grope her. In time she realized she was asleep and became more daring in charging into the dark rooms, but she knew it would be dark where she woke and in such she was afraid to wake up, too. It took her many rooms to develop the courage to rise, and she found herself sitting and leaning her back into a pillar that held up the hospital entrance awning. A film of snow had developed on the sidewalks by the time Camila arrived, which left Embree shivering. Winter's teeth were settling in.

"Are you alright, sweetheart?" Camila asked through the open passenger window.

Embree lent her a desperate gaze while wearing the sagging, hand-me-down, red and blue hospital sweater and pants.

"You pull it off, you know," Camila said.

The ride home would be a litany of lit side streets and unlit back roads and snowflakes coming at them like stars at warp speed. Embree palmed the cold window and let her hand slide down, squealing. She began to cry.

"Bree, how are you holding up?"

"I can't even remember the accident. All I know is I lost

my best friend."

Camila was naturally a peppy speaker, but she lowered her voice to its softest, saying, "Let's celebrate his life tonight, Bree—to Jason," while raising a cupped hand. "Landon's out on call, thank God. We pretty much have the place to ourselves."

In the outskirts of the town of Triangle, Camila stopped at a liquor store, ran in, and from its unadorned warehouse-style shelves selected a bottle of Vodka and paid up front, where they handed it to her in a brown paper bag and slid to her the change, all as Embree waited in the passenger seat of the pickup, with the engine still running.

Before heading home, they stopped at the Triangle diner—one of two trucks in the small parking lot. Inside the diner stood a pool table, a few circular dining tables and chairs to the side, and a row of barstools along countertop stretching for the almost the length of the room. One fat man stooped over a sandwich at the far end. Camila and Embree perched side by side, and a young Irish-looking woman—pale, freckled, and light haired in the dim diner lighting—approached them from the other side with a faux smile that Embree could tell was for show.

"Hi! Can I start you guys off with something to drink?" she asked, sliding them menus.

"Water, please," Embree choked as the waitress listened and watched, unflinching.

"I'll take a Labatt tall," Camila declared, swirling her hand through the air to take the attention off Embree.

The waitress walked to the back.

"Gotta pregame," Camila whispered, leaning into Embree.

The waitress walked back with a bottle, popped the cap, took a glass mug from underneath the counter, stretched out a long hose and pulled the trigger over it until cool water almost kissed the lip, added a straw and lemon wedge, and somehow without spilling slid them both to Embree and Camila.

"Are we ready to order?"

"I'll take the taco salad special."

"I'd like, umm," Embree stalled, "a fried fish sandwich, extra tomato and tarter, please," and she took a deep breath, soaking in the relief of freedom from that terrible, confining place.

"I'll be back with you in a few minutes," the waitress said, again walking back.

"Jason was a wonderful person," Camila muttered, leading Embree to sigh.

Fifteen minutes passed and in both hands the waitress came out balancing two oval plates of food, the smell of which drove Embree wild. They dined in near silence amid the beauty of the fish mounts and all-seeing deer mount on the wall.

"Let me pay, Camila, after all this you've offered me," Embree said, insisting and handing the waitress a debit card, signing and writing a thirty percent tip on the receipt, and handing that copy of the receipt back. They left, packed, and on their way out the cold was jarring but also seemed so much less awful.

Gray-green pods of firs and hemlocks passed from their view among the groves of barren oaks reaching over the road and a few elms touched lifelong by Dutch elm disease. As they pushed into the countryside, great escarpments of crabapple and twisted, snow-dusted vines bordered the roads. This was the start of the wilderness of upstate New York holding wild dog packs, bobcat, fisher, bear, and snowshoe hare, all of which Jason once hunted.

They pulled down potholed Hattie Clark and into a long driveway of stone, dust, and snow. Camila's house had a dreadful grill, doormats, and some children's toys strewn across the porch, but Embree had higher hopes for the inside. "What do I have to lose," she thought. A child cracked open the front door and peaked through at cross-armed Camila and Embree making their way up through what had turned into a heavier snowstorm. The trails of Embree's tears stung cold in the gusts, and she winced and covered her face with her forearms.

"Embree, this little spying monster is Lorenzo, my son. He'll be eleven soon, won't he?"

The dark complexion of Lorenzo's face disappeared from the crack of the doorway.

"He's a little shy."

They could hear his galumphing laughs from a back room and the escaping pitter-patter of his short, quick strides. The entryway was of dull beige rug with duller plastic matting and old, steam cleaned circlets of piss stains every few feet—the family room. The couches were old but refurbished, and the TV sat small in its stand. Fruit fly shit trimmed the upper edges and corners of each room. They wandered to the kitchen. A thin, black Siamese cat perched atop a charging laptop on the cluttered kitchen table for heat, and Lorenzo came back running headfirst toward them.

"This is Ray, our cat. He's sick. Lorenzo, say hello. This is Embree. She'll be staying with us for a while."

"Rat, get off the table!" Lorenzo spat, picking the bony

cat up and plopping it on scarred linoleum.

"Lorenzo!" Camila barked, raising her eyebrows, "say hello!"

"Hola," he muttered, rushing off again.

Fruit flies burst from the greasy stove burners and the kitchen sink drain as Embree paced about the room, holding her re-bandaged arms out and spiraling about a center island loaded with cat treats, painting supplies, and a garbage can. The countertop had a microwave, ancient toaster oven, and stacks of pots.

"I can't wait for him to become a teenager," Camila said, droning on. "Anyway, this is the bathroom," she said, holding out a hand, "and over here is our spare bedroom."

An undressed twin bed lived among strewn weight-lifting equipment; a toppled bookshelf; and piles of sweaters, shirts, and pants.

"Thank you. Is Landon okay with me staying?"

"I don't give a shit what he thinks. It's my house."

The squall outside melted and stuck into the mesh screening of the windows, within which many house flies and squash bugs had been trapped and starved and piled near the edges.

"It's a dirty house, needless to say," Embree thought, "but it was awfully kind of Camila to take me in," and she smiled for the first time in a while.

Camila motioned her back into the family room and to a couch where they sat together with the vodka.

"So what's on your mind, Bree?"

"I wouldn't even know where to begin. The days are so long, and I'm haunted by so many things. Where can I even begin," she said, holding back her tears.

"Well, at the beginning, honey."

"I keep seeing Jason; I see Rod and my mother. I see them, rotting. I hear them, screaming. For better or for worse."

"Honey, what are you talking about?"

11

Embree woke upon her mattress from a honeycomb of complex nightmares, shuddering, to the clack and grind of a key being jammed into the front door.

"Cam, I'm back," Landon shouted through the opening, dragging a loaded cooler behind him. "Take a look at these puppies."

Camila sauntered in disheveled from bad sleep as well and pouted, licking her teeth, laying into him with her words. "Shut your fat mouth. We have a guest. Let her sleep."

"That's more like it," Embree thought, smirking and diving backward into her cocoon of blankets.

It was Saturday and after some coffee Camila had settled into her usual cheerleading. By afternoon Embree had finally risen. Landon had cleaned off the center island and was slowly filleting steelhead and the piebald, almost rotten carcass of a snagged king salmon. He had Camila fooled in his manliness, but Embree could tell by the strokes of his knife that he was a fair-weather fisherman at best. She made no comment, however—simply looming and observing, pokerfaced, and eventually she walked away.

By midafternoon Camila and Landon had decided off to the side to have a grand bonfire to welcome Embree.

"Bree, how about we have a bonfire and finish the vodka tonight?" Camila proposed.

"How about you finish the vodka, and I take as many Tylenol as you'll give me," Embree whispered back, palming her head.

"Two. I'm a nurse in training. You get two."

Outside, the fencerows of old barbed wire stretched long into the hills, straddling and then distancing themselves from a woodlot that almost butted up to the house and a small, cattail-choked pond. Only a few young aspen clung to their brown leaves, rustling in the breeze. Camila, Lorenzo, Landon, and Embree walked together to a fire pit alongside the pond with its ash and gray nuggets of charred log reaching out from the middle.

"Lorenzo, go collect some kindling, buddy," Landon instructed.

Landon with his bulky arms hauled split logs in sevens and eights from a pile skirting the house to the fire pit as Lorenzo came back with three twigs and chuckled.

"Lorenzo, you got to put in your part here."

"You can't tell me what to do!"

"Uh, I've been your stepdad for three years—absolutely I can," Landon said, raising his eyebrows and staring the child down.

Camila nodded, agreeing reluctantly.

"Huh-ha! I wanna mushroom hunt!" Lorenzo exploded.

"Not by yourself, honey," Camila said.

"I'll go," Embree added, seeing Landon's sly look. "What? That sounds interesting. And we can get some more sticks for the fire."

"Mushrooms are fucking disgusting," Landon said.

Embree and Lorenzo wandered into a narrow forest of mystery with its crunchy beds of dead leaves dusted with the last shadowed sleeves of snow from the night before. Logs crisscrossed through the firs where some had toppled during high winds, and a grove of heavy oaks lived to their left, where they headed.

"Do you find them often?" Embree asked. "And what do you do with these mushrooms, Lorenzo?"

"Ha-huh!" Lorenzo cried out again. "Eat them, I guess. That's what the guy on TV did."

"Do you know some are poisonous?"

"No," Lorenzo said softly. "Here, cross here," he said, pointing at a lattice of sticks over a small soupy creek that wound down through the forest from a pipe where the pond overflowed.

"Mister yells at me when I fart," Lorenzo added out of the blue, "but a lot of times I do it and they don't notice, ha-huh!" and Embree laughed at his honesty with nothing to add but a smile.

"Whao," Lorenzo said as the sticks cracked under Embree's weight, yet she chuckled and continued to hop across.

"Mushroom thingies!" Lorenzo shouted, pointing.

At the base of the grandfather oak, in the crevice between jutting roots, stood a hoary gray-brown contraption like the fronds of a palm tree but also twisted like the antlers of an atypical monster buck into a round, almost brain-like blob.

"Lorenzo, don't eat that shit," Embree sighed, intrigued as she was.

Embree knelt and scraped at its fronds with her fingernail. It was firm and desiccated, and spores drifted from its fronds as she continued.

"Landon has a point," Embree thought, circling the base of the tree to look for another but simply finding leaf litter, acorns, and a sifting of snow.

Near the great grandfather oak was another fallen oak

and along its back side she noticed a majestic mushroom: gray and dull orange in color, with thick fronds like shelves layering sideways along the length of the tree almost as if a colony spanned nine feet.

"Whoa," Embree said, amazed. "Lorenzo, look at this."

"That's like one on TV!" Lorenzo yelled, running over and reaching for it; it was wet, melting off and falling to the ground in half frozen chunks as he poked at it.

"I think it's dead, Lorenzo. I'm no expert, and I have no idea whatsoever if they're poisonous, but I think all these mushrooms are so rotten that you'd get sick even if they weren't toxic."

They knelt and, finding pockets without snow, collected a bushel of moist kindling between them and returned to Camila and Landon, who were sitting in two of several lawn chairs bickering amongst themselves. They poured the kindling atop a generous pile of crumpled newspaper, and Landon leaned in, lighting a match. The sun dipped fast and to the west behind a smooth November cloud, and against the gaining fire one light traded for another, violet-blue eaten by blood red.

"Camila, Landon—I want to potty," Lorenzo said, tugging at Camila's shirt.

"It's pronounced 'Mister,' Lorenzo," Landon corrected. "Mis-ter.'"

12

The next cold morning, well before sunrise, Landon and Embree rose to go steelhead and salmon fishing in Pulaski, which they had agreed upon with Camila late in their drunken night before. Embree at first had hesitation—honestly, who could she trust so soon?—but her balkanizing mind in the moment began yet again to long for the gambler's high and the gambler's peril. In the darkness they found the world blustery, howling, and unpleasant with early morning snow flurries rocketing sideways in bursts. Landon and Embree took trips from the garage, carrying a duffle bag of fishing gear and other comforts and stout, long spinning rods loaded with twelve pound mainline and each dressed with a breakaway split-shot leader and fluorocarbon down to a snelled octopus hook. They loaded the fishing rigs and bag over the flaking rust of the pickup's edges and across the bed, reaching.

"Gonna be a bear of a morning," Embree said, "but I'm just happy to get out." She sighed.

"It's too windy," Landon said, shaking his head, but still almost instinctively he pushed about and fitted the gear in the back so the tips of his poles weren't propped or otherwise bent, for against his wishes and better judgment he was going.

"You're such a pussy, Landon," Embree thought. Aggravation well beyond what was called for welled up in her chest as stress, and she continued to carry it—like the antithesis of a little lost love in her heart—with her without speaking.

The drive to Pulaski was dark and foreboding in the

underpowered and close-range yellowish view of the headlights. A gray fox a little bigger and puffier than a housecat bolted across their view, but they said nothing until the back roads were history and until they had moved onto the northbound highway.

"Bree, what exactly happened with Jason? I know you and Camila talked about it, but..."

Embree remained silent, crossed her arms, and closed her eyes, leaning into the old seams of the truck seat with the back of her throbbing head; yet again, vodka had gotten the best of her.

Pulaski was the sort of town where you'd imagine a small motel murder scene or imagine a mall erected and dying within ten years. They arrived by five in the morning, and Landon knew the two-way traffic on the town's potholed roads was ninety-some percent anglers driving back and forth and inspecting spots where many anglers had already parallel parked upon the side of the road and hiked to the wooded river, waiting. They stopped at Chunky Chinooks in the dark, and the expanded parking lot was a beehive of activity within which they barely found a slot to park. The ride had been quiet besides the offset-sounding churn of the engine and rattle of the paneling.

"Come in if you like," Landon said, slamming his door.

Inside were massive lines of fisherman—some scuzzy and less clean shaven and many loud and most in waders—leading to the few cashiers who hurried to process the morning's peak activity. People clogged the aisles, bending over and kneeling to look at overpriced salmon beads, egg mesh, egg sacks, hooks, line, leaders, weights, and other terminal tackle. A fifty-five-pound Chinook salmon mount jutted from the wall high above the entrance among archways of smoothly processed logs used as struts, giving the place a log-cabin look. Landon waited in line for fifteen minutes to buy a small pack of pink salmon beads for eight dollars.

In the lot, Landon found Embree leaned back and napping with her mouth ajar and tongue rounding over her lower incisors, snoring. He was gentle with the door and sorry for prying earlier, but it was past the time where he could comfortably apologize, and now he had to live with it—buried deep in his gut where only time could mend it.

They drove by the ballpark where already almost fifty cars formed a long parked procession in the park grass, as Landon saw their silhouettes in the predawn glow.

"Who deserves to slip through the cracks? My father does. Rod does. Jason didn't." Embree dreamt such that the words echoed throughout her head. "Do I?"

Sunlight began to bleed past the slate-gray nimbus clouds of the east. The flurries had died down.

In time, they arrived on a busier street and parallel parked beside the pizza joint in one of the last few free spots, and Landon woke Embree, who looked at him angrily. They stepped out and suited up in waders that were tucked in tightly behind the bench seat and grabbed their equipment from the bed and began a quarter mile hike along the sidewalk, skirting the whole way the bumper-to-bumper vehicles of anglers that seemed to line the street endlessly. They made their way to a bridge where eleven people stood and looked over at a giant oval of silhouetted anglers forming below—three hundred yards long by one hundred yards across at the widest, the anglers themselves a giant fish trap—and the seeping sunrise lit the wakes and riffles of the headwater a dim and silvery navy blue. They had arrived at snaggers' paradise: the town pool.

Making their way down the giant rocks and finally the mesh-caged wall placed for erosion control, they walked the shoreline down, far down, until reaching one open pocket of fifteen feet near the back of the oval but still along the side. Most people were casting out a bead with split-shot on spinning rigs, ripping the rod back once, and then reeling in the rest of the way; some were ripping over and over without care or regard to the rules. Salmon and steelhead were jumping and slapping the water near and far, hooked in the eyeballs, fins, and ass and desperately trying to shake the hook, making fast, reel-burning runs up to the head of the oval and darting back down over and over.

"Fish on!" and "On!" and "Hooked up!" and other alike phrases shouted time and again from the fat lips of the fisherman up and down and across the oval. Their early morning pep and politeness was showing, and most resisted casting over the lines of those fighting fish that had rocketed far up the oval, tautening the monofilament mainlines to their breaking points, wherein the luckier anglers stood no chance in getting the fish in once others had crossed their lines. It was a shit show of humanity, and the worst was yet to come.

"Ah, Pulaski—asses and elbows," Landon said.

People were nearly shoulder to shoulder, maybe a foot apart in the thicker spots with a few waiting along the shoreline, with the growing stringers of light red coho, zombie kings, and striking silvery pink steelhead all behind the wading anglers. Landon fought three fish and lost two to the hook popping off, finally giving Embree some instruction.

"Embree, do it like this. One hard pull back, then reel it in the rest of the way. Not more than one pull though. That's illegal."

She ignored him, thinking, "I'm not interested in snagging, pussy. I thought we'd be fishing."

Upon netting his second salmon of the day, Landon noticed Embree had softened up a little as time outdoors is a great relaxant, and she had her eyes on him and began to pay attention to the details of his dance. He got on his knees and wrested the hook out of the gut of the salmon, which had come in sideways and belly-up when the bystander netted it for him, and she let the stress of the situation well up once again in her heart, adding to that of before.

"That salmon's gut hooked," Embree said dimly, looming. "Nothing about any of this is legal."

"That's why you have to take it out fast," Landon said, referring to the hook.

"DEC on the bridge!" someone yelled from across the river amongst the other shouts and clamor, but Landon was too far down from the bridge to be concerned, concealed in his unhooking by the crowd.

By afternoon, Embree and Landon had broken into their duffle bag for snacks and water, and still they didn't speak. She felt as if she had a hot coal beneath her sternum from the aggravation. One angler with a centerpin waded further and further past the contour of the oval, twenty feet past, to the point where he was standing where a young boy at the bend of the contour had been casting.

"Hey, asshole, move the fuck back; my son's been casting there all morning!" the burly, curt father hollered.

"I can't reach out that far," the old man said back. "I'm using a centerpin." He whipped the rod back and forth as if he was fly fishing.

"I don't care what you're using! My son was here first."

The old man backed up and sloshed ashore and laid his shoulders into the caged stone wall well behind Embree and Landon, waiting—but what for? He struck a match and lit a cigar.

Embree finally felt a tap while reeling and whaled up into the fish, snapping back her rod, and she let out a "Woo-hoo," taking a deep breath. It jumped: "a fresh, gorgeous steelhead more rebellious than her or Jason or both of us combined," she thought in so many words. Across the way and down the line fat-mouthed fisherman began to holler at her.

"Hottie's got a fish!"

They catcalled.

"Whore's got a fish!"

Instantly her demeanor lost its last spark of excitement and hope and she leaned back her head with the reel zinging and heating up in the brisk November breeze and let them all know with a shout: "Fuck off!"

"Oh, we got a feisty one!" another angler shouted back. The catcalls continued.

The steelhead with a speed and ferocity she's seen in few saltwater fish and none freshwater shot up the way past forty anglers wading, jumped again, and slapped the water directly in front of a distant man who recoiled and brought his forearm to his face. The afternoon attitude had devolved into every man for himself, and about half of those forty anglers while watching Embree casted over her line selfishly, and a grand knot began to form in the middle where all the lines had slid together after hooking hers.

"Come on, you fucking morons! Don't cast over," Embree cried. "You, cut your lines!" she said, pointing while perched atop a tall rock.

"Show us your tits!" Embree heard from the rowdier group across the river.

"Yeah, cast another one over it; fuck it," Embree said.

Embree flipped all of them off and began heaving, reeling, and pulling until the grand knot had met her top eyelet and jammed into it. Nobody had cut their line and all that had snagged her continued to pull, too. She felt a smack against her ass, and—twisting back harshly, gasping, and hopping down from her perch—she saw a teenage boy among friends backing up from her and laughing. She turned back quickly and threw the pole ahead into the deep blue of the hole where it dipped and skipped across the surface before sinking reel-first, pulled by the fish and all the connected lines webbing out from the knot at its tip, and she turned back and screamed so loudly her voice cracked: "Do not fucking touch me!" She charged forward as the jock kid backed up, his hands in the air, smiling, and she lurched forward and swung at his face with a right hook and all her strength, adrenaline coursing. After she connected like lightning with his jaw, she shook her hand and screamed. He continued to back up, blinking and opening and closing his jaw again and again, reddening at the left of his face where his trimmed beard ended and bringing his palm up to hold it. His friends and Landon and Embree became tangled in a war for one another's arms, trying to restrain each other as they grunted and she screamed, until all five found a standard-issue glock pointed at the middle of the group, and they settled and stared.

"DEC, break it up," the plainclothes officer said. "Where do you get off slapping a girl's ass like that?" he asked the one.

The kid took a short breath and, trembling, he shrugged.

"Shit," his one friend said.

"Were those salmon snagged?" he asked, pointing to Landon's stringer.

"Of course they were," the ass slapper said.

"I didn't ask you, kid."

"No," Landon said.

"Well, I didn't see you catch them one way or another," the officer said, eyeing him up and down. "You, you, and you, come with me," he said, pointing at the teenagers and gesturing up and away from the river with his weapon.

Embree's pole was long gone. The grand knot had snapped several times over, and those who were connected were now on their knees rummaging or standing and retying their rigs. Nobody had landed that steelhead—too many cooks.

"You lost my fuckin pole?!" Landon said through his teeth, head down and eyes raised such that that his pupils tucked under the crest of his brow.

"We're leaving," Embree said, staring back, expired by the eyes.

Embree grabbed the stringer with its two salmon and heaved it over her shoulder, feeling the strain of the taut rope and wetting what little of her shirt was exposed over the chest waders. She climbed a set of washed-out roots, rising to a forested dirt trail, which wound its way back to the main road. Landon followed reluctantly with the duffle bag and his rod, his stout figure like a gnome beating back the branches.

In a private parking lot, Embree found a scraggy, unshowered man leaning into the guard rail. She wanted nothing to do with him, and he reeked of pot even from a distance, but he began to speak and, out of some shred of politeness she had left, she stopped to listen.

"Yeah, the DEC was on the bridge, man, and they was picking out all the people snagging, and one of them walked down and gave all the snaggers tickets, man."

"Must've just been at the head of the pool," Embree said, sighing and walking on. The smoker kept talking even as she fell from earshot. Landon had passed her and would have the truck running by the time she arrived. She heaved and slapped the salmon into the knuckles of the truck bed.

The ride back was silent for the first half, and Embree wondered about her future—near and far—to the point where she began again to cry and choke on her little gasps of air.

"What's wrong? I'm sorry for getting pissed back there. I didn't mean to get angry at you. I just—I was tense."

Embree nodded while crying.

Back at the house, Embree laid into her mattress for the afternoon, cried, and rolled in her discomfort trying to find the right position. Her headache reemerged; the soft pillow felt hard almost immediately. She was restless, getting up and pacing about the room some hours, playing miserable hopscotch around the floor's magazines, piled furniture, weightlifting equipment, and Lorenzo's scattered toys. The resentment from earlier, and earlier yet, burned low and for the most part remained concealed in her chest.

By dinnertime, Camila had heard from Landon of Embree's hardship for the day. She knew Embree was in the spare room for hours, sulking and sleeping, so she'd prepared a special dinner of angel hair spaghetti garnished with red sauce, cheese, and fried green tomatoes before checking on her and rousing her from the mattress.

"Hon, it's time to eat if you want."

Embree strolled into kitchen where Lorenzo circled the center island hyperactively, dancing and pirouetting as he went.

"Mister, when are you gonna be done with those fish?" Lorenzo asked.

Landon hung over the center island and cringed at the question, slowly and deliberately peeling back the fillet and working the knife in small strokes.

"I'll be done the day you stop asking questions, you ADD twat."

Camila glared at Landon, and Embree stomped over to the kitchen table.

"Rat, get off the table!" Embree barked, picking up and plopping the cat on the floor.

"Hey, you can't do that to him," Lorenzo said.

"He's not supposed to be on the table. Shut up you little bastard."

"Embree!" Camila cried.

"What?!"

"What are you thinking? You can't talk like that to him."

"Why don't you fuck off?" Embree shouted, picking up a porcelain salt shaker and throwing it into the wall, denting the drywall and watching the piece explode.

Embree opened and stormed out of the front door without thinking, spiraling in a red-hot fury, slamming the door behind her, and feeling an attitude in the cold wind on her skin, an attitude not unlike her own. In socks, jeans, and a sweater borrowed from Camila, she began first to walk, then run, across the snow-dusted grass of their front lawn; through the ice-slushed ditch that soaked her socks; across the street; and into the shaggy, twisting hickory and crabapple before anyone could think to look out the front window and try to spot her.

Past the crabapple thicket, the parcel expanded into an extensive meadow hundreds of yards deep. Old goldenrod stalks and a few tufts of hay poked from the ground here and there among the odd crabapple clusters and a peninsula of hardwoods extending up and into the meadow. A late woodcock flushed from a pocket of saplings with its constant tweeting and corkscrew flight.

Embree's feet felt a cold burn at first, soaked since crossing the culvert, but she was resolute and delusional and panicked and simply wanted to die but wasn't sure how and didn't want to commit to it herself; she somehow wanted to die naturally, then and there.

As she approached the wooded edge, dark in form yet bright in-between with the shades of snow-dusted bark, Clicky startled her, coming from the burl of a grandfather oak, but still she marched on, finding a tall stump, which she climbed and sat on Indian style, shivering.

The entire meadow had been a downhill crawl, but the forest dove sharply ahead of Embree—part shale-encrusted hill and part sheer cliff—diving fifty feet down into a gorge where a half-frozen creek snaked through.

Embree sat perched atop her throne for a while, sobbing, gripping her feet for warmth and repeating the words from the day's conversations over and over nonsensically.

"Why don't you fuck off," Embree whispered.

Broken and confused and lightheaded, Embree descended the cliff and crossed the cracking ice of the creek at its edges, hoping she'd fall through and freeze to death. This chance brought her comfort and entertained her. Tiptoeing one small step at a time, she breathed and let out a shivering sigh time and again, for with no recourse from anyone else, she was letting the comfort consume her. In time, when snow showers turned to sleet, the little wet crystals piled atop her shoulders and pelted her scalp.

Embree's face soured. Delusional, she tried to climb the opposite bluff, grabbing at roots that pulled loose, dirt that broke free, and rocks that pried out like rotten teeth, first working her way up ten feet, pressing her body whole into the frozen edge. She swung from a hemlock sapling that hung from the cliff, hearing it crack at its base but bending enough to bring her gently back to the creek. She slid along its icy edge in her socks, spying the tumultuous riffles that never iced over between her icy bridges. Finally, the cracking ice gave way, and she fell through, soaked up to her knees and gasping, and she fell forward and grabbed the broken edge, almost falling through completely. She belly crawled out like a troop under fire, eaten alive yet not knowing yet what true suffering was.

Embree didn't notice the sunset, but the woods were

fading quickly and harshly in the thin November air. She climbed the cliff, curling her toes to grip the rocks, and returned to her stump, sitting Indian style again and shivering violently. She peeled back a sock to find her petite foot lightening.

In the vanishing daylight, Embree found a grove of young firs between the meadow's and forest's edges and pushed into it, confused and exploring for a cure. The trees were bedded in circles of yellowed needles, the snow settling on the ground in lines in-between. She crouched and stalked through the pines, bending back the boughs, unsure of whose property she was on but straying in thought and interested. A small, square foundation of sticks appeared in an opening along with an old beer can propped up on a stick—perhaps a property marker. She pushed on until finding a winding trail in the pines, which led her to another meadow, and she spotted within it another house with its horse farm and a man moving hay bales from the back of the barn to the front, so she skulked backwards into the pines again.

Emerging from the head of the pines, Embree could see through the sleet and so much crabapple the headlights of a truck peeling out from the house of Camila and Landon, and she knew it was them, looking for her. She figured after they made their rounds on the back roads that next would come the cops if they were daring enough, and, screaming at the skin, she still had just enough clarity to know she did not want the cops involved.

Embree's stomach growled, but this was the least of her worries, if she had any. Life had devolved into a sad and unlucky joke. She scuffed with her numb toes and feet through the slosh of the sleet in the hay until she finally reached the road, hundreds of yards up the way. The stones of the road stung deep and oddly in the soles of her feet as she marched back toward the house. It was dark and she found two trash bins at the base of their driveway, where it met the road, and she pushed them together and laid across their tops, calm and collected and thinking she was trash.

Landon hit the brakes hard as he approached the driveway, turning in and parking. Lorenzo was in the passenger seat, without Camila.

"Embree," Landon said tenderly, holding out his hand, "can I touch you?"

"No, never," Embree sighed. "Nobody can t-touch me anymore."

"Come on back inside with us, please. We can work this out."

Embree agreed and slumped into the house where Camila stood cross-armed and clearly unwilling to compromise.

"Camila, we found her."

"I see," Camila said. "And are you sorry?"

"I'm," Embree stuttered, shivering still and barely able to speak in a low soft voice, "I'm not—I'm n-not the one who s-should be s-sorry."

"You don't speak to my boy that way, puta!"

"Ladies, please, stop and sit down," Landon said.

They collected in a tight powwow in the kitchen, the chairs facing inward in a circlet, and breathed themselves calm, Lorenzo with his hands folded, until Embree restarted.

"I need a f-fucking blanket, p-p-p-please."

"Stop swearing!" Camila shouted.

"Camila, what has gotten into you?" Landon added, "Settle down!"

"Yeah, M-m-mila."

"Stop it, Embree!" Landon said, standing up and letting the chair squeal back and tip over.

"What are you g-gonna do, Land-y-y? There's n-nothing you can d-do to hurt me, absolutely nothing, even with all of your strength!"

"Fuckin shut up!" Landon said, trying to assert his dominance.

Embree laughed hysterically, loudly, and without a care for anything whatsoever. Moments in, she switched, and holding up her hands she began to weep, and the tears streamed down her frosty face.

Nobody knew how to react to Embree. Landon, and even Camila, began to feel a pity for her like nothing they'd ever felt for anyone, and, beginning to understand her irrationality, they tried to soothe her with their words.

"Ok, Bree," Camila said, "why don't you have some of this special dinner I made you, get some sleep, and we'll sort this out in the morning."

"Yeah," Landon insisted, finding a blanket and laying it over Embree.

"Are your feet okay?" Camila asked.

"I c-can't feel them," Embree muttered.

"Let me take a look."

"No, I don't want anyone to touch me ever again," Embree said, putting her hands to her face. "I fucking don't. I don't. Don't—I do not."

"Ok...honey."

Embree ate the cheesy spaghetti first by picking under the topping of fried green tomatoes and, fork in-hand and trembling each time she brought it to her lips, saved the treat of fried tomatoes for last. She crashed on her mattress after changing into warm, fresh clothes, still shivering and deep red now at the hands, heels, and toes.

In the middle of the night, Embree threaded on triple socks, double pants, triple sweatshirts, and she up and left with a duffle bag she found in the spare room that she had filled with more clothes. She was quiet in her escape, closing the front door so gently that the latch wouldn't startle even a watchdog.

"Soy la puta reina," she whispered back at the door.

PART 3

13

As Embree marched the backroads, and despite the layering of socks and her shoes, her feet were raw and red and sore from narrowly dodging frostbite earlier in the evening. The night was colder and darker and gustier than she expected, although she asked God for no favors, and her head was empty of hope and wanting. She marched out of habit of strength and working through the tougher times, she marched to escape, and she marched for she had nothing better to do.

"Jason, why'd you leave me—where'd you go to? I needed you," Embree thought, mouthing the words over and over.

Embree had a vague idea of where she was going. The moon was a thin sliver floating over the southern horizon, or so it seemed to her, and starlight lit the first few feet of crystalized mud in front of her scuffing shoes. She kept her hands buried in her pockets.

Embree walked Hattie Clark for forty minutes before reaching that smooth pavement of Route 12. She remembered a few pertinent things about the area from long-ago conversations with Jason: a little river, the Tioughnioga—"or was it the Tiogniogh," she thought—flowed through Whitney Point and was fed in part by the lower Otselic river, which flowed from the reservoir; a deep, winding, oxbow-loaded river, the Chenango, swallowed the Tigarniogh and lazily ran south where it met at confluence park with the Susquehanna river; and, finally, around that junction was the large, Hell-frozen-over city of Binghamton, from which she figured she could travel almost anywhere. She remembered from the recent coming and going that Route 12 roughly followed the Chenango river down, and, even if not straightly and directly, it at least eventually led to Binghamton and its surrounding cities.

The pavement was kinder on Embree's feet, and she walked the highway's shoulder, crying again. Route 12 was long and unforgiving, she knew, and an orange and black dump truck with double bladed plow grating the pavement loudly and its circling yellow caution lights blew past her, spraying her with an arc of icy slush from the plow and then its spray of salt from the rear. A slow train of cars followed the plow truck, one beeping at her. She spat the gritty salt from her mouth. Patches of her left-side sweatshirt layering were moist now to the touch, and she knew in time the wetness would wick down to her skin.

"Route 12 is too long to hike," Embree thought. "No doubt Camila will call the cops, and the cops will find me after sunrise."

Still, Embree trudged on, too alienated by the world and its people to hold her thumb out for a ride. She thought about it, however, but what would she say—that she's on the run? How would that blow over, and would the driver use it to try to take advantage of her like the others? She feared the soft touch of any hand, like that of her piano teacher back in Gloversville where she sat on his lap as a child and learned to fear. Northbound and southbound headlights of cars and trucks sped past her by the minute, their tires splattering through the salty mix.

Within the hour, Embree saw the tall yellow and orange lights lining a Mack truck, and she heard the whine of its brakes and growl of its j-brake, watching it slow in stages until by her side, hissing. The driver rolled down the passenger window.

"Whatcha out here for, boy?" the man said, trying for a tart-voiced quip.

Embree lowered the hood of her sweatshirt and shook out her long brunette locks from the collar. Her face was a gray-yellow silhouette in the dimness of the caution lights.

"Goddamn—oh, sorry miss, and curse my mouth," he stammered. "Do'ja need a ride? You can'ch be out walking in this."

Embree said nothing and stalled for a moment, collecting her thoughts and breathing in short huffs. She reached and grabbed the handle of the passenger door and locked her shoe into the stirrup, unlatching and rising into what she reckoned was the lesser of two bad decisions. The bench seat of the eighteen wheeler was of old, cracked leather that squished beneath her sitting, and behind it was the dark cabin where the chubby, mustached man wearing ratty flannel and jeans slept away the off days.

"How long have you been—?" he asked in a soft voice.

"Too long," Embree interrupted. "I've been walking for too long. I've been hoping for too long. I've been living for too long."

"Wow, okay—where do you want to go?" he asked.

"Where are you headed?"

"Cleveland," he said.

"That sounds like a miserable drive."

"A little bit at a time," he said. "That's how everything gets done."

He had moved the truck out of neutral and was now merging back into the traveling lane, gearing up the truck as he went. The soot of the street lit dull and yellowish in the headlights, beyond the brow of a dusty dashboard with its inset speedometer and other white, red, and orange lit meters.

"So you're headed to Binghamton then?"

"Through there, yes ma'am," he said.

To Embree, the drive felt long and monotonous and confining as she sat trapped at speed with such a strange man. Cars whizzed by in the dark passing lane, sometimes putting on their turn signals and shifting in front of the truck after going by.

"What's your name, mister?"

"Rod," he said softly, his eyes dead set ahead.

Embree scrunched her face and sighed and suffered goose bumps for a moment, and for a while it was the time of greatest quiet and reflection for her. Heat billowed from the vents of the dashboard.

"Well," Embree said, "thank you for caring about me enough to stop."

Embree felt a soft touch upon her thigh in the dark for just a moment, then gone, and she gasped, mouth agape, and looked down to see the silhouette of a hand groping about blindly.

"Beer, I need my beer," he said.

Embree found him his beer from a cup holder and thrust it toward his portly, balding head, where after a few seconds he saw and grabbed it.

"Thanks," he said, "...honey."

"Out," Embree said, holding up a hand. "I'm out! Stop the fucking truck."

"Jeez, alright—I take it you don't want a beer then?"

"No, fuck you," Embree spat, jumping down and slamming the door behind. "I'm not going to be your roadside date rape!"

The truck started off again in slow huffs between gear changes, with two blasts of its horn signifying something to Rod, Embree thought.

"Why does this keep happening?" Embree thought. "How many motherfucking times do I have to say I don't want to be touched before the world stops touching me?"

"Did you hear that, everyone?!" Embree shouted into the dark ridge of carved stone alongside the highway. "I know you can hear me, fuck!"

Turning, she saw the endless lights of Binghamton and Johnson City in all of their glory, and she became giddy, smiling and laughing and skipping down the highway's shoulder for a quarter mile, following the bluff until it faded back and an exit appeared—taking that down to a junction of thoroughfares and expressways circling into one another and the arterial streets with their streetlights by a closed gas station and down the way so many tenant houses.

Four streetlights down, and already once again cold, Embree saw what she eyed from standing by the bluff above: the nightlong lights of a Walmart. She wandered the crisscrossed roads, brushing past the little raised wood-chipped plots of planted firs used as medians to divide the roads from the parking lot, and on her way to the sliding doors with their great swell of heat she passed a homeless man dressed in black and crouching by a shopping cart, head against knees. She took his cart as she walked, unflinching when his head rose.

Inside, first she passed the greeters, deadpan staring them back. Then, she passed the registers; the pharmaceutical aisles; the children's toys and bikes, passing so many degenerates and their twisting, crying, out-of-hand children; and finally turned into the outdoors section where stood an island register station with its state-issued hunting and fishing pamphlets and its lower glass cabinet of knives and its upper cabinet of guns. Beyond that, one aisle was loaded with locked-away ammunition of most every type and rows of airguns and machetes and camping gear while another was rich with all the fishing tackle she could hope for. She grabbed a flint and striker; a grill lighter; a sleeping bag; tarp; cording; a machete; one fillet knife and one pocket knife; knife sharpening stones; a tent; two light fishing combos; two spools of monofilament; hooks; weights; split shot; bucktail, curly tail, and swimbait jigs; other expensive hardbaits; and, from the kitchenware aisle, a few pots and pans and some cardboard cans of salt, tossing and piling them all into the cart. She was for the most part clearheaded and thorough; she planned as if this was to be her coups de grâce, her final trip.

At the register, the melancholy attendant raked all the items past the laser, sometimes twice, and bagged them in gray plastic bags. T he total came out to $232.43, which Embree paid with the debit card in her otherwise empty wallet, raising her eyebrows at the cost and thinking and finally figuring she had just over a dollar left. The cart was hers, too, she decided, and she walked out the sliding doors.

"Spare change?" asked the middle-aged homeless man.

"You should be paying me," Embree said, walking on.

14

Jason's words from years ago echoed through Embree's head: "I basically grew up on no-man's-land by the Susquehanna. You can do anything there. JC Goudy down to Murphy's island and down further, miles...and some other spots if you look hard enough, too."

It was almost midnight and the traffic slowed around Embree, who walked the street with her cart through the slosh of the salty ice and past streetlights dirtied from summer insects and spiders. Still, nobody fully stopped for her. She took a break, leaning into a guard rail, using the last of her phone's battery to open a map application and zoom in on Johnson City and Westover, studying the grid of city streets. She would take Lester Avenue to Main Street to 17C, past all the perpendicular roadways connecting and past the exits leading to and from the 201 Bridge, and finally she would take Avon Street and Elbon Street to its end. She was two miles to freedom, and she grew lightheaded and wild in the eyes, skipping again as she pushed her cart with all its stores and the duffel bag. Even at midnight, the interstate was a hive of big trucks, pickups, cars, SUVs, and most everything in-between.

"Reina," she thought.

Embree hadn't known much Spanish from her studies, but it was the crude, jesting lines from classmates that stuck with her and stuck with her well.

"Two miles, reina," she thought.

Embree sweat from her feet into the tight layering under her shoes, and by now the wet mix from the snowplow had completely soaked in and stained Camila's sweatshirts with splotches of brown, cooling her comfortably and not yet freezing her. She could hear the nighttime coos of a pigeon flock perching in the structure underneath the bridge; though, staring up, she could neither see them nor the beams they rested on.

"Everything in little steps," she took away from the truck driver, thinking.

Squeaking into the urban zones, Embree followed her heart past the dilapidated two-story tenant houses of Johnson City with all the junk collecting on their porches and their switchback stairways snaking up the sides. She could see the silhouette of the great smokestack of the retired Goudy Station power plant reaching toward the stars, and at the end of Elbron Street was the fencing with barbed wire where still in the days—only God knows why—workers with their government pickup trucks would enter the power plant and chain and lock themselves in.

At Elbron Street's end, William Hill Park was beautiful and simple in the falling moonlight. A sign of the hours and short drive led to a parking lot, barricaded by posts and chain from the great swathe of mowed ballpark grass surrounding it, on which a lot-side gazebo stood. Already, Embree could smell the septic from the sewage plant outflow a mile upstream. She knew the river was near— perhaps opposing the hedgerow at the far side of the grass. She pushed her cart over the soft earth of the ballpark and down the way where the river drew near to a tall berm behind Home Depot, following a trail until she met woods, and she knew in her heart and gut that this was it: this was the start of no-man's-land.

"I am the queen bitch, and this is my kingdom," Embree hollered into the dead night.

Embree left her cart in the woods and, unboxing and pocketing the smaller knife, decided to go exploring in the heat of her overblown excitement, which was something she never wanted to end. Her arms ignited with radiant energy that seemed to flow out as the sun. She ran for warmth in the film of her cooling sweat, crossing back over the grass and culverts along the trail, around another berm at the upper end of the ballpark, past its rock-loaded drainage ditch, and it was then that she spied the strikingly handsome and complex and noxious Goudy. To her left, in the dim moonlight, Little Choconut Creek spilled beyond the berm through the woods and around a metal barrier and those rock-cage erosion control blocks. Past that, the Susquehanna roared over an old, broken metal-and-concrete dam, bordering the wooded bluff and splitting in its whitewater and wild curls and wakes around a rocky island before ending up near the beach by her—the shallow riffles. Far away was the railroad's aged trestle bridge and, far beyond that, the faintly silhouetted bridge of Route 201. She could see the wandering of flashlight beams over the concrete of the dam.

"I miss the fireflies," Embree thought, skipping about the shoreline.

The trail followed the contour of the creek, dropping off sharply at times as a root-crusted cliff, and up the creek—where it was rather deep and full of microwaves, shopping carts, bicycles, and so many limbs and other wood—a thick metal pipe, shiny along its top from the tiptoeing fisherman, connected one side to the other. Embree balanced with her arms out and a smile, making quick work of the pipe. She climbed the soft incline of the other side past dying stalks of Japanese knotweed to a platform that overlooked the Goudy in its septic splendor—a walleye factory, by Jason's assessment, which she had always trusted. She leaned her belly hard into the railing, raising her arms, and she took in the starlight, eyeing Virgo and Sagittarius and Arcturus.

"...and this is my kingdom," Embree softly said.

Coyotes howled and whooped along the river's other side, two hundred yards across to the opposite shoreline and down quite far, almost to Murphy's Island. Still, it sounded to Embree like they were much closer. She crouched through the archway trail of knotweed surrounding her like a dense, browning jungle without steady form, some parts thicker than others, and crossed down a shale bluff bordering a great graffitied metal wall that ran alongside the dam. She hopscotched around the shoreline rocks until climbing the gentle concrete incline of the dam, and suddenly the flashlights were on her.

"Damn, you snuck up on us," what seemed to be a man said.

"Who are you?" asked a woman.

"That's what I do best," Embree smirked, gripping the knife down in her pocket.

They turned off their flashlights before Embree could make out their clothes or faces, spying only their outlines in the starlit night. The man sounded as if he was mid-twenties in age, and so did the woman.

"We're Dan, Sandy," the man said.

"Embree," she cheered back.

"And I really don't care who you are," Embree thought.

"We're fishing for catfish," Dan said.

Embree knew already what they were trying to do by the starlit propped poles buried into the gaps between where the steel met the concrete of the dam, and she guessed by the coldness of the season and the look of the pool and current ahead of them before the island that they were failing. The catfish simply were not there.

"See, we got a system," Dan said. "Sandy, show her the system."

"Dan takes his empties and takes some line off the spool and sets them on top of the line—here, like this," Sandy said, pointing toward the shadows. "That way, when a fish takes line out, we hear the beer can fall over."

"Oh, neat," Embree said. "When's the last time you guys caught a catfish?"

"About a month ago we got fifteen on chicken liver and hotdogs," Dan said. "We've got nothing yet tonight, but you never know when they're gonna come by."

"Figured as much," Embree thought.

Embree walked the dam back and forth for a while, straining to climb over the roots of a grandfather oak that had fallen into the river in the last storm and settled over the concrete. On the other side, she found the concrete craggier and metal rustier until the walkway ended abruptly at a manhole, the water flowing in a trickle over it, before the dam veered left and then strait again, and the water thundered over its edge. In the curve of the waterfall's flow, the remnants of green algae swayed underneath like mermaid's hair with its phosphorescence.

Eventually, Embree climbed back over the oak where she found the couple chatting quietly and drinking, crushing the empties, and trying to skip them across the river. Dan turned a flashlight on again, and first Embree could see their army backpack with all their possessions, and then Dan aimed the light at Sandy's face, then his own briefly. Embree was perplexed and slackened at the jaw at the sight of their faces, which seemed to her old, rough, and pitted; they appeared fifteen years older than they sounded, at least. After a minute of confusion and after they had stowed the flashlights away and continued chatting, she had realized they must be addicts and stewed in that thought for another minute before approaching them again.

"That bridge, up there," Dan said. "I ran across the top of it one day."

"He did, too!" Sandy howled.

The crisscrossed silhouette of the steel trestle bridge caught Embree's eye in an entirely new light, and she spoke with the giddiness of a toddler.

"I'm gonna go do that. Watch me!"

"No, don't," Sandy said. "If you fall in, you'll freeze to death."

"Oh," Embree said, smiling. "You don't know the first thing about me. I am death."

Embree ran off and jumped across the rocks jutting from the rippling shore and climbed the bluff like a spider monkey, twirling her way through the knotweed jungle this time up and away from the dam, breaking the few late cobweb strands that haven't been touched in so long, threading her way up through the brown stalks and avoiding the sinkhole that once was a groundhog burrow along the narrowing trail, rounding the corner of the power plant's barbed wire fence, and finally seeing in full the great outline of the trestle bridge.

Embree climbed the large rectangular foundation stones like those of the pyramids and tore at their browning vines to reach the base of the bridge, which was a railroad bridge and accordingly was laid with wooden slats and gaps in-between carrying the girding of the rails along its length and off forever into the knotweed thicket. She walked half the bridge, and the cold breeze made an appearance, whipping past the hood of her sweatshirt. She tried at the beams angling into the night sky as the sides of great supporting trapezoids, hugging and inching her way up the frosty steel and flaking rust until she was twenty feet higher, slipping up recklessly to the top, where she stood and waved at whoever in the night might be watching through the starlight or maybe from far up above. She tiptoed across the beam, holding out her arms.

On her way back down the trail, Embree found drunken Dan and sickened Sandy stumbling and slipping up the bluff with their rods and all their belongings strapped to Dan's back. She took their rods for a moment and offered them a hand, and Dan showed how often he shut his mouth.

"I was here in the spring," Dan said, "and I was having a hell of a day—musky, pike, walleye, bass—but the DEC busted me for fishing out of season here and gave me a ticket. I guess you can't fish before walleye season opens here—bunch of bullshit. I'm the king of the Goudy. I can do what I want."

Embree could feel the heat of contention rising in her heart and pumping through.

"Well you better move over," Embree said—and with that note, she turned back, crouched, and disappeared into the knotweed abyss.

15

The following morning was unseasonably warm, and Embree had worked her way along with her shopping cart, forcing its wheels through the wet earth and tangles of scrub, traveling farther down no-man's-land, passing the deep trenches of river behind Home Depot and beyond the clay banks where the river split around several islands in rushes and riffles, reaching down past where the forest broke and to a scrubby meadow opening between the river and an elevated highway that ran along no-man's-land handsomely. By midmorning, she had stripped down to a t-shirt and jeans and bare shoes, hanging the sweatshirts and socks on the lowest limb of one lone silver maple in the brush. She found the sunshine warm and the breeze cool and refreshing. She hadn't slept, but still she felt rested and eager, her soul afire.

Embree laid out all her purchases in the morning's melting frost atop the matted hay. She began to unbox and assemble her tent—her kingdom's castle centerpiece—and fit the tent poles together with the tug of the elastic cording connecting them and wrestling to jam the tent poles through the slits of the tent's fabric, finally with base poles in and upper poles crossed, realizing the blue round-topped tent in its freshness and splendor. She entered and rolled around about the floor in excitement and ran her palms along its smooth sides.

The trail leading to Embree's camp was forged by deer and summer fisherman—virtually nobody walked it in late fall or winter or even early spring. She could hear the vehicles from the highway, herself urban yet rural, almost in sight yet truly alone, and in that she found comfort. It's not that she wanted to be alone, but her hand was forced. Who could she trust?

"Fire, food, shelter, water," Embree said. "Or is it water, food, and then shelter? Yeah, it's gotta be that one."

Embree thought back to the few televised survival specials she'd seen as a child as well as her book, but they were of little help now; her memory was failing her and so was her ability to concentrate. She paced in circles about her tent, restless, until remembering minutes later what she was doing, and she strolled through hay, dying dandelion, desiccated thistle, briars, and willow saplings, pushing back the branches past where the trail had ended, before she found where the forest of mostly great silver maple regained its prominence down the way. She picked at the leaf litter upon the still-frosted knoll, finding and bundling twigs and midsized branches against her chest that had fallen in the last storm. Beside the knoll, a small, cold, maple-leaf-covered swamp basted and rotted any wood that fell into it.

Embree made trips back and forth, trailblazing and collecting a mound of frosty sticks and leaf litter tinder that she was proud of before unpacking her machete and working it with the sharpener until it could shave the hair from her forearm. She found herself back in the forest hacking away at a small fallen beech tree, swinging left and then right to cut chips from the slit she had dug into the wood, and by the time she was sweating, the log had split and collapsed into itself. She chopped half the tree into manageable pieces, carrying them out and back to basecamp and piling them neatly beside the tent, each time wiping the sweat from her brow.

Embree slid through the thistle of the clay banks on her ass, scooting like a crab, pot in hand, and at the bottom, on a narrow level path of wet clay with its raccoon and opossum prints, she knelt and filled the pot with the rushing river water. She reached deep off the shoreline's edge, grabbing dozens of rocks from the freezing river bottom and hurling them to the top of the bank.

"Ouch, the water's so bitter," Embree thought, shaking her hand.

Embree knelt and then slowly crawled back up the bank, balancing the pot of water in one palm like a waitress. She took the stones scattered in the weed growth one by one and walked them over to her tent, fashioning the border of a fire pit alongside. She took the tarp, spreading it and unfolding it by shaking its corners, and she tossed and worked it over the tent. With the machete, she took her time to sharpen four sticks thick like her thumbs, then burying them deep into the edges of the tarp where it met the ground, pinning all together tightly, and finally, with her pocket knife, she cut out from the green tarp an arced entryway complimenting the tent's zipper. The cut edge of the tarp was frayed. Within the tent, she shoved in her sleeping bag like a field mouse's tousled nest.

"Boil the water first," Embree thought, but she hadn't drank since before her blowout at Camila's house and was so thirsty.

The tinder had moistened from the frost warming in the strong sunlight. Embree tried to make a pile of it in the pit, throwing sparks at it first with the striker, then torching it with the grill lighter, but neither worked immediately, and she grew aggravated and soon after drank from the pot of water raw.

"There, that was easy," Embree thought. "Fuck you, fire."

Embree paused, soaking in the sunlight, leaning into the heels of her palms and breathing, and for a moment the spirit of the world and its ragweed grass and archway briars seemed all the less cold.

"Food," Embree thought, pondering.

There was one way which Embree had trained to catch food, and that was through fishing, but she knew in the back of her mind there were many other ways to eat, even if these ways didn't come to her mind's forefront right away. She took off her shoes and sat in the grass with her legs out and, taking a stick, stuck it through the spool of line and cut the plastic wrapper off and unspooled some line and tied it to a bare fishing reel with an arbor knot. She held the line against the pole with one finger and stuck the stick holding the spool between her toes, adding tension by squeezing her feet together. She reeled, and the spool spun until the line burned through the bend of her index finger, and she kept reeling still for minutes, loading the reel with line and then cutting the line from the spool with her teeth and threading it through the eyelets of the pole and finally tying on a jig to the line's free end.

Embree slipped with her pole down the clay banks to the head waters of a wicked run, shallow but ripping with a current break along the far side and its sheer drop-off on her side where she earlier picked the stones. She jigged for forty minutes, popping the rod back and reeling in slack, covering every stretch of the run over and over, and she finally felt a tap and ripped the pole back so hard the fish broke the surface immediately. She horsed in the small walleye where it lay flapping aimlessly on the thin stretch of clay bank on which she stood.

Embree filleted the walleye boneless in a matter of seconds against a stone. Staring down the damp fire pit, she bit into the fresh and bloody flesh raw and ravenously, and her incisors ached from the coldness of the fillet, so she huffed and breathed past them between bites for warmth. The flesh tasted plain and dull and a little dusky, but it was firm like thick gelatin. She ate both fillets in a few minutes and drank with them the unclean river water from the pot.

"Is this sashimi or sushi?" Embree wondered.

That afternoon, Embree's guts knotted and ached and she had a spell of diarrhea while exploring the forest beyond. She spread her cheeks and pissed at the same time, relieved. Time healed her bellyache. She felt a pinch on her knuckles, and she found the year's final mosquito, fat and translucent with blood, taking advantage of her. She swatted it flat and smeared it across her skin.

"Fuck you, fire," Embree said again.

The night fell cold and crisp with a burgundy sunset past purple cirrus clouds. Embree wrestled with the fire that evening, tediously drying the tinder with her grill lighter before the fire finally took. She built the fire with sticks and logs gradually and also positioned two tall, flat stones within the circle of the pit to hold over the fire the boiling pot of water. The fire roared and crackled with orangish flames and a bed of red embers, casting her shadow after sunset across the face of her tent. She slept comfortably in her soft sleeping bag in the tent, even long after the fire and its embers died out.

The following day, Embree stuck to her developing

routine, except she had her period and cut a rag of linen shirt to wear under her jeans, and for all her misfortune on this godforsaken planet, she sighed a spell of relief for never becoming pregnant from being raped. She explored. She stepped cautiously and patiently through the frost-bedded forest and wooded marshland, making her way a mile downstream along the river, past beaver slides and squirrel nests, before reaching the hard-packed dirt, weed tufts, and interspaced maple of no-man's-land's end. A short trail appeared beside a cove and rope swing along the river, and she followed the trail up a hill and to a gate, past which she dragged her feet over the parking lot and down River Road, spying cottages and a Victorian house and all the signs saying "Walleye season closed from March 15 through the first Saturday in May" and posted signs riverside signed by the bitch living at the end of the road, who Embree already hated and felt persecuted by, just upon seeing her signature. Stress welled up in her heart.

Embree scuffed down the road's shoulder for what felt like most of a mile, and she reentered the forest where the barren road bent back toward the highway and the posted signs ended, stepping into a new swathe of no-man's-land with its drying knotweed jungle in-between maples. She crossed Patterson creek, crawling up the other side of its great gulch. Beyond, quad and dirt bike trails wound through the forest. She followed the trails deeper and found dirt mounded into jumps, twists, turns, and halfpipes as tall as her for as far as she could see, all swallowed in forested meadow and many laid with a puke-green ragged carpet for grip. She wondered how such an abandoned park could be made without a bulldozer, which never could have passed between the trees.

In the expanse, Embree spied a barking squirrel clinging to the side of a maple, and she could almost see below its rippling skin the nourishing muscles, on and on staring; this led her to think about how she could catch it. Strolling through the stalks of knotweed, she saw, first in glimpses, then, walking up to it, as a whole, the chassis and engine block and slate blue paneling of an old shit Chevrolet half-buried and clutched in late brown vines. Tassels of wiring coiled about struts and through the car's cavities and over the rusted battery terminals. She gawked for a moment, tapping her fingers against muddied denim, then started ripping and cutting with her pocket knife long and short strands of wire, bundling them all together into a great multicolored knot before heading back, inspired.

At basecamp, the morning sun shone white off the frosty grass, scrub, and weeds, and at times Embree shielded her eyes but still tried to soak in nature's glory. In an instant, her mood dive-bombed; she spiraled quickly into deep depression. She held the fillet knife to her wrist, sat in the cold clumps, and cried for some time, comforted by the pinch of the blade against her skin and the promise of escape.

In time, Embree raised her head and stopped weeping and soon after stopped sniffling. She untwisted the bundle of wiring and laid out the wires neatly in matted weeds beside the fire pit, experimenting. She grabbed her coil of cording, unwound and cut three feet of it, and pulled free all the thin, loose strands from the cording's material sheathe, splaying the ends out in her palm like a bouquet. She took one thread, which she could feel and guessed had a breaking strength of around seventy pounds, and tied its end to itself with a polymer knot, forming a noose of sorts, and she stripped down the coating of the wire with her pocket knife and tied the other end to the wire's copper with another polymer knot, looping the copper end back around several times for strength. She held up the stiff, arced wire with its paracord loop: her first snare.

Embree made ten more snares for a total of eleven and tested the connections, tugging each taut. The paracord loops were short but the wire leaders were made long so she could tie them off to a tree or drag. She wandered through the desolate part of no-man's-land, snares in hand, tying the first one off to a chewed-off sapling stump and positioning the loop to one side of a beaver slide. She tied others by their wire ends in the willow saplings that clustered between the forest and highway berm to the side of the marshy edges where rabbits had made obvious runs. A few she tied and propped along low limbs for squirrels, searching hard for and finding and balancing acorns on either side of the loop for good measure.

Embree returned to her tent, zapped by the earlier depression and shuffling along before crawling inside and resting. The tarp kept the harsh sunlight out—the dark predator's den.

"I'm gonna build this castle up tall, so very tall," Embree thought.

16

Embree had gained all with time without faring well. A hard month and change passed. The frosty ragweed was buried in inches of snow, and even river riffles had iced over. Her castle was a masterwork of large logs bracing one another, crisscrossed with paracord and capped with snow, forming a tall fence around her tent and cart and fire pit and the magical barren spot where she sometimes laid and reflected and cried. The trail into no-man's-land, spider-webbing into the abyss to every snare set used a dozen times over, was a trench of hard-packed snow. Beside her tent stood a pile of almost thirty frozen walleye like cordwood that she'd fished out before the ice came. Strung between the fencing were the tails of many rabbits, gray and red squirrels, and even the flat leathery blackjack of a beaver tail drooping heavily in the middle.

Sometimes Embree felt as if she was having a heart attack, an aching in her left ventricle like a stone being hung from her heart, and she welcomed the pain and the hope of passing on unexpectedly, but after long hours of laying and moaning it would usually subside.

One afternoon, when the winds were howling and snow flurries fell sideways, Embree woke from her depression sleep and laid in the tent for some time, comfortable to the touch and crying, before unzipping her tent and stepping into a freezing desert. She wore all the sweatshirts at once all the time and smelled of body odor, cheese, and blood, often itching her scalp and picking at her greasy, windswept locks.

"I'm a monster," Embree thought, looking at the heap

of squirrel, rabbit, and beaver skins and sniffing her armpit. "Look at me. I'm fucking worthless. Can I do anything right?"

Embree did what she did best in her world, and that was hapless meandering. No task was in order; she had a routine of sleeping, checking traps, boiling water, drinking, cooking, eating, and shitting, but the order of that routine on the daily was subject to change. Often she was bored and she found boredom to be the ultimate killer, the leading generator of stress and suicidal thoughts where she'd slit her wrists and light up the snow, so on the day of the flurries she took her machete and fishing gear and walked the forest and iced-over marshland most of a mile down to River Road, where the water slowed and pooled beneath a sea of staggered ice floats and where Murphy's island began.

Far onto the craggy, crackling ice, near the industrial complex of Murphy's island, was a hunched-over man fiddling with his ice rod by a hole and beside a tackle box and hand-crank auger. Embree avoided him. She avoided him for loathing his existence and the fact he was near her island, in her space, persecuting her.

Embree tiptoed along the concrete slabs and frosty stones leading down the shore's ridge, moving awkwardly onto the slanted, frozen-together ice, which clogged the river, with her arms out, balancing gear in-hand. She waddled far onto the ice, closer to the head of the run where it dropped off, she could tell, as the current break alongside it broke through the ice, bubbling.

"La tristesse durera toujours," Embree thought—the only French she'd ever known or cared for and that she heard that time at the art gallery in Manhattan while on a field trip.

Embree slid to a stop and plopped down her rod and tackle in its gray Walmart bag and took swipes at the ice with her machete, leaning left and right with her swings, shaving away—the ice chips spraying free. She found the ice where she was cutting to be three inches thick, but she truly didn't give a shit if it was ten or an inch or a half. She could only imagine the glory and relief of falling through and tumbling down the current underneath until her lungs burned.

After the ice gushed open, Embree stood back and dropped the jig from her overlong pole into the cerulean-gray depths trickling past the uneven hole. She popped the jig, with the line slanting back gently with the flow of the water. Past the glare, she began to make out a face, like that of a pale drowned man, but eventually she realized it was Clicky down there, rippling, and she looked up, ignoring him. She jigged for half an hour, squinting sometimes at the old man on the distant ice, half to make him out and half out of contempt. She felt no taps, but the tip of her pole began to bend with her pulls as if she caught bottom, somehow and suddenly, and then the pole bowed harder and the drag began to click as line drew out, first slowly and soon after almost setting the spinning reel afire with a fish's hellish runs. She stuck the tip of the pole into the water so the ragged ice wouldn't cut the line, and over the minutes—the fish burning upstream and tipping sideways, writhing, and doubling back and racing downstream—she kept her composure and back to the man so he wouldn't see, but then in what seemed like a moment he was on top of her.

"You got big fish!" he said.

"No shit, old man. Why don't you mind your own business?"

His face was taut, pitted, and light brown, and he wore a pom-top knit beanie; he was clearly of Laotian descent, Embree thought. He stepped closer, grinning. He didn't understand.

"Gaff?" he asked.

Embree rolled her eyes but waved him near with her free hand.

"Gimme that fuckin thing," Embree insisted, holding out her hand and raising her eyebrows and motioning with her fingers.

The man handed over the worn, wood-handled gaff, and Embree knelt with her rod buckling and near breaking in the grip of just her right hand as the fish neared the hole, twirling and thrashing underwater and showing itself in glimpses beneath the overcast sky and still amid the wind and flurries. The fish was long, tan, and striped, gleaming in and out of sight. It lumbered, tired under its own dead-weight and porpoising, especially as it drew closer to the hole. Her rod was bent nearly into itself.

The fish finally gave up by the hole and floated into sight like driftwood as Embree lifted the rod tip from the ice, and first its side showed with a white iridescence between ferocious and numerous light brown stripes, the line still angled off to the side as she held it with her gaff-gripping fingers such that the line wouldn't cut against the ice. The drenched line guides froze over in the winter wind, and she knew she had no more play and that this was her one chance. The duck-billed, shimmering head glided into view under tension threatening to snap the line, and with one quick onehanded stroke she gaffed the tiger muskellunge in the eyeball and skull and wrested it with two hands out of the water head-first, throwing her pole and grunting.

"Nicest fish! Fifty dollar!"

"Huh?" Embree said, sighing.

The fish worked side to side, belly down, sliding along the slants of ice, its maze pattern and rust-orange fins mesmerizing to Embree, who'd never caught any sort of muskellunge before. It was forty-some inches long and twenty-five pounds, by her estimate. The ice crackled beneath the party's weight.

"I give fifty dolla!"

"Oh?" Embree said, smirking.

The man pulled out a leather wallet that was too fat with bills close from the back pocket of his jeans, fingering through the money and pulling out a fifty. Embree held out her hand for a handshake and the man stared back for a moment, then obliged, smiling. She took the crisp bill.

"My name Sy."

"Embree," she said. "You know, I have walleye back at camp."

"Wall-eye?" he pronounced, beaming.

The tiger muskellunge's eye was flat and bleeding and drooping out of its socket, and, watching the last moments of the delicate fish as its gills froze and fangs frosted over, Embree had a flash in her mind that had been buried until now: Jason's brains hanging from the back of his head, smooshed, along with thick red streaks ornamenting the guard rail, and she cringed and gritted her teeth and sucked through them the cold air. She held her forehead, massaging it.

"Yes, wall-eye," Embree said without looking at any

particular thing. "Go back to your hole and wait for me. I'll be back."

"Wait...here?" Sy asked.

"Yeah, whatever," Embree said back, flashing a hand.

Hiking, Embree spotted a halo of the sun through the clouds past all the drifting flurries and silver maple reaching with their bare limbs. She met basecamp in twenty minutes, and she kicked at the stack of frozen walleye until it broke from the ground in two great chunks. A few walleye were left frozen to the ground, but the deer mice had gotten to them with their under-the-snow tunnels and chewed at the fish's heads a little, so she'd save those few for herself anyway, she thought. She bound a strip of cut shirt around each hand like mixed martial arts wraps, and she balanced one clump of walleye in each hand, huffing more than anything from the weight of her intrusive final thought of Jason.

Embree wormed her way back through the dead wilderness, mad at Sy for figuring he left already and aching from the coldness of the fish drawing through her wraps, and she walked the expanse of ice clog. Sy was still there. He had dragged the tiger musky to his near-island hole, and in its time-of-death pose, like a mounted deer, the flurries were beginning to stick to it.

"One hundred dollars!" Embree shouted, walking up on Sy and letting the clumps crash into the ice nearby.

Embree was exhausted. She held her knees and panted, with greater and greater breaks between breaths. Smiling, Sy broke out his wallet again and handed over two fifties, which she wadded up and pocketed. She could see he was packing up, having caught and kept for himself only one small yellow perch.

"Come," he said—"help," as he dragged the muskellunge and waved Embree toward shore.

Embree rolled her eyes and pawed at the freezing walleye again until she had them balancing on her wraps, and she crept across the ice and then the crunchy, snow-packed forest owned by the bitch, cutting across to Patterson creek's no-man's-land, following Sy. They walked up the creek, crossing over thin ice and through trickles, up the cement skids lining the walls of the overpass, and finally they broke from the scrub and around a construction site's fence to Sy's green hatchback on the dirt shoulder of Argonne Avenue. He opened the back without unlocking and heaved up the muskellunge with its solid, sagging gut, throwing in his gear too, and she tossed in the bricks of walleye and tried to catch her breath.

"In," Sy said, pointing to the passenger door.

Embree looked at him, confused.

"I've done enough favors for you, old man," Embree said. "Why the fuck do you think I'll trust you all the sudden?"

"Food," he said.

Embree was spent and hungry and tired to the point where she was almost dry heaving. Reluctantly and while holding the grip of the small knife in her pocket, she entered the back seat of the hatchback where nobody could touch her.

"I won't make the same mistake twice," Embree thought.

Sy drove Endwell's grid of streets for a minute and a half before parking along the right curb in front of a beige townhouse with miniature ceramic blue elephant and orange lion statues guarding the porch. He hollered from the front lawn in a dialect of Lao, and his wife and then son came out to greet them. They chatted in Lao.

"Hi," said the older woman, smiling with her teeth staggered like a stepladder.

"Hello, I'm Sip," said the son. "Dad says you helped him get a bunch of fish?"

"Yup, that's me," Embree said. "What do you guys want so much fish for?"

"He is a leader at the local Buddhist temple. We share it with the community."

"Oh," Embree said, softening.

"Come in," Sip said. "We have snacks from the temple."

Inside was a host of men, women, and children, everything from Laotian neighbors to extended family, standing and milling around and talking to one another in English and Lao, but not loudly enough where Embree could follow any one particular conversation. Some stared at her. Sip brought an ornamented bowl full of cracker packs, baby whole zucchini, and sticky rice and bean patties wrapped in plantain leaves. Over half an hour, she opened and ate everything out of the bowl, sitting on a chair alongside a table where Sy and others knelt.

"I'm a fucking heathen and these people know it," Embree thought, growing paranoid again. "These are the nicest people that've ever hated me."

17

On average, Embree slept back at basecamp for sixteen hours a day, and these hours could be during day or night or both. She walked to Walmart from basecamp under a midnight meteor shower, scuffing her feet and making cold fists and staring up. She took a cheap red grill, plopping it in her new cart—*hers*. Half the shoppers stared at the spattered blood and mud on her shoes, jeans, and outer sweatshirt. She found the sliding doors leading to the separate gardening section, enjoying the waft of warmth every time she walked through a set of those doors, and, planning ahead, she grabbed the little seed packs including strawberry, garlic, peas, zucchini, and rhubarb. This was the home she never had, she thought, and without the contention that had always been there, and she would treat it that way and build a garden and become more than the queen of death.

Back at basecamp, Embree watched the roof of her tent from the softness of her sleeping bag, which had frayed at the seams over the start of the long winter, and she watched as Clicky and Vinny and what seemed like a reaper, with his bony forearms and scythe, haunted the roof of her tent, emerging from its darkened face in form and closeness she'd never seen, drooping down into her gaze. Sometimes the screaming would suddenly continue, sounding like it came from just outside the tent, and this is what truly startled her. She would flinch every time it happened, whether children's scream or adult's.

"It'll all be over soon," Embree said, hoping.

That night, Embree thought of her love of Jason—his

rebellious but, for her, caring nature and how her best times were behind her, but what was ahead? Everything could be over in a moment, she knew, cringing, and that would wrap everything up nicely. She had seen it firsthand—not so nicely—and she had felt it when touching Jason's hand for the last time in a delusional daze, she suddenly remembered, and how the warmth had left him for coldness. She couldn't remember the sight, only the feel.

Embree fell asleep under the howling wind tearing at her tent and tarp, and she suffered nightmares and night terrors, first of Jason disowning her, then of the light switches again not turning on and the monsters around corners trying to take advantage of her, and finally of a leper screaming and hurling itself toward her. She woke in a fury, rolling into the side of the tent and hitting her head against the tent pole and punching it three times.

Embree could see the penumbra of forest's dawn seeping through the tarp, but there was something more, like a searchlight, flashing in streaks past the castle of logs over the tent's side, and immediately she sat up and thought of the cops, but how would a police cruiser flash her with its scanning spotlight—from the highway?

Embree unzipped the tent and tripped, falling knee-first into the snow, and suddenly in the predawn glow she heard the crunching of the snow, and soon the flashlight was on her. The coals of her fire burned a dim current.

"Miss?" said a man, blinding her with the flashlight.

"Surprised you can tell I'm still a girl," Embree said back, squinting and holding her hand to her brow. "Are you a cop?"

"DEC officer," he said. "Quite the impressive place you've got here, and quite the pile of skins," he said, scanning. "Can I see your license?"

"What license?"

"Well, how did you acquire all those skins and tails?"

"They just appeared there one night," Embree said. "Most amazing thing."

"I need to see your trapping license," he said.

"Didn't know they existed, sorry. How did you find me again?"

"The coals—you can see them from the highway," the officer said.

"Damn, you have good eyes."

"Do you have an ID?"

"Here," Embree sighed, reaching for her wallet.

In the light glinting off the ID she could see what looked like grenades or something just as sinister strapped down the front of his army green bulletproof vest; a glock on his side, where the silhouette of his hand was resting before; and a dark police mustache spanning his portly smirk.

"Embree?" he said, sounding to her confused.

"The one and only."

"That's a beautiful name."

"Thanks?" Embree said.

"Okay, so, Embree—all these here," he said, reaching into his pocket and drawing out some snares, "aren't legal for trapping in New York, and you need a trapper safety certification and trapping license, too, and even then, these still aren't legal, honey."

"I'm sorry sir, but what'd you expect from me?" she asked. "I'm homeless and I need to eat."

He paused, letting the flashlight beam fall to the ground, and he held his chin, and after a while he spat some chew spit to the side.

"Okay, what's your story?"

"I'm too sick to work, and I can't count the number of times I've been left to pick up the pieces."

"Sick with what?"

"Mild bipolar or something like that, to quote my wonderful, all-knowing doctor."

"Okay, honey, I'm sorry. I'm gonna cut you a break," he said, sighing and pausing. "And I'll help you out, but you've gotta take the rest of the snares down and stop setting these snares all over the place. I'll be back later. You'll be here, right?"

"Yes, sir," Embree said, shaking at the hands at this point.

There was something off and nerve-racking in the way the officer presented himself, Embree knew, and in the brokenhearted sunrise she could see the back of his black and army green outfit and the gray streaks in his brown buzzed hair. She hoped he would never come back, but wishes were just wishes. She thought of burning the place down and moving on; if it was still summer, she may have. He cut through the willows quietly toward the highway, and in a moment he was gone.

Later in the day, and to Embree's surprise, beneath cirrus clouds and in the blinding sunlight the officer returned with plastic bags of groceries in hand. He came insistently, silent in his approach but clearly visible against a background of sunlit snow in the distant stretch of silver maple. She was standing outside the castle, waiting for water to boil.

"Oh God, here he comes," Embree thought — "motherfucking fire."

"I brought you groceries, sweetheart," the officer said.

"Please don't call me that," Embree said back. "I'd rather 'queen of the Goudy' or 'queen of death' or even 'that bitch' over 'sweetheart.'"

The officer chuckled in his deep voice, setting down the groceries on the snow. In the bags were fresh fruit, vegetables, finer cuts of pork and beef, candy, breads, condiments, and sweets. She leafed through them.

"Thank you," Embree said.

"Anytime, honey," said the officer. "Did you pick up your snares?"

"I will soon, promise."

"Okay, good."

While picking up her snares, Embree found one squirrel struggling in a snare by the thickest maple of no-man's-land in a hollow, caught by the waist and chewing but only able to reach the strand of wire, and sadly she was figuring this would be the last animal she'd kill on her trap line. The sun cast shadows from the limbs above on the snow. The squirrel contorted itself backward, biting at the wire and grunting. She took her machete and with one dramatic slice chopped into the neck of the squirrel, severing the spine, and the squirrel collapsed immediately with its eyes stuck wide open.

At basecamp Embree skinned, gutted, and slow cooked the squirrel on a spit over the fire, basting it with barbeque sauce brought to her by the officer. She rummaged through the bags. The meat was frozen in finer vacuum sealed packages. The condiments were brand name. She bit into an apple and tasted the sweetness for the first time in so long, ringing against the bitter of her mouth. The officer had gone all-out. She dug with her knife through the tough squirrel meat after it cooled and while the coals were still glowing.

The following day, Embree was depressed and bored and coped by snacking on the oversweet candy and napping. She followed her trails out to where the snares had once been and found another set of prints going to each one, sized like the officer's, but the officer was nowhere in sight.

A week passed and the world only grew colder, with temperatures going negative at night and on one occasion up through midday. Embree was often cold in her sleeping bag, napping the days away, but she tried to at least keep a steady fire close to the tent to cast warmth onto the fabric of the entryway, and with that she had to keep finding, chopping, and carrying dead wood. Her food stores dwindled, and she often wanted to try ice fishing again, but she worried about the consequences of being caught. Eyes were on her now. She grew deeply paranoid, at times trying to spot the officer and always failing.

By the next day, Embree had run out of food and was terribly hungry, napping and crying on and off, when she heard the light crunching of the snow and plastic bags rustling again. The officer walked up to her with a cheerful smile, groceries in hand, but still she held her fists in her pockets as if she was cold, but secretly on the right she was gripping her opened pocket knife for insurance.

"Hello," Embree said. "Thank you."

"Oh it's no problem, honey. I got you more this time. Where'd you get that grill by the way?"

"I found it. You wouldn't believe the shit on town land."

The officer got uncomfortably close to her, close

enough to elbow her, and he dropped the groceries within the arced fence of the castle, and they crashed into the snow. She took a step back. He held out his hand and touched the top of her shoulder, smirking.

"Embree...," the officer said. "You know what I think?"

"What?" she said, trembling.

"That you're a filthy girl."

With that sentiment Embree tore her right hand free and, with an awful grimace and a grunt, plunged the knife toward the officer's neck, but he was fast to step back and, unholstering his pistol, the knife landed in his bulletproof vest hard enough to bend the thin blade. He continued to trot back, raising his gun.

"Hands on your head, knees on the ground!" the officer shouted.

Embree dropped the knife and folded into herself, falling to her knees, raising her hands to her head and crying.

"What the fuck is wrong with you, Embree! After all I did for you, you can't do anything in return?" yelled the officer.

"I don't want to be touched," Embree said, sobbing.

"Lay down on your stomach, face in the snow, and cross your hands behind your back, and cross your legs," said the officer.

Embree followed the officer's instruction and the snow stung against her trail of tears and wind-burned chin. She saw packed snow and the shadow of her own face instead of the forty-caliber muzzle of the pistol. Her head was spinning.

"Not the time, Vinny!" Embree shouted into the snow.

"Poor, crazy, filthy Embree," said the officer.

The officer strolled over and straddled Embree on his knees and cuffed her with one hand and, with the other hand, pushed the muzzle hard into her back. She screamed.

"Remember, Embree, nobody will believe a crazy homeless girl," the officer said.

With that final note, the officer reached underneath Embree's tight waist, feeling the skin drawn taut and cold against the snow, and he undid the button of her jeans and unzipped her pants, sliding himself back and drawing them down. He worked down the same panties she'd worn all winter, and she screamed senselessly and kicked with her heels at his back.

"Damn, you are a filthy girl," the officer said, chuckling.

Later, he uncuffed her, leaving faint redness and bruising on her wrists from her writhing. He stood up, his one boot planted firmly on her ass, and he began to simply walk away, holstering the cuffs in their special slot. Embree's crotch was numbing at the front and aching at the back. She didn't move, save for her gasping. When she finally looked up, he was gone.

"Jason was right, fucking pig!" Embree spat into the all-seeing void.

18

Over the following days, Embree slept, sobbed, and gradually consolidated the pillars and novelties of her castle into one great pile, and around midnight she took the grill burner and lit the tent fabric sticking out afire. The drying tinder caught next, and soon the logs and cording were smoldering, catching, and finally blazing with a roar that would challenge any beast.

Embree stayed for just a few minutes, weeping and crossing her arms and backing up as the headache-inducing heat spread, before charging toward the Goudy—nothing in possession except a knife, grill lighter, wallet, pack of clothes, one fishing rod, and a few jigs.

Half an hour later, at the head of William Hill Park, Embree could hear the fire alarm and whine of the sirens making their way down the highway. She took Elbron Street down, past all the little lawns and above ground pools covered over for the winter and the switchback tenant houses—the salty slush of the snow's shoulder wetting her shoes and the cuffs of her jeans as she marched—and she rounded the corner onto Avon street, walking it down to 17C where the big trucks, sedans, and cars burned by, splashing her with slush.

Embree explored, taking the exit uphill to the 201 Bridge, panting and suffering from a headache. She kept having flashes of the rapes—more of the feel of confinement and pinching and tearing pains than the sight of it—and with each of these she would wince and mutter to herself. As she walked under the streetlights of Highway 201, she thought of climbing the short concrete walls and jumping from the overpasses to the highways far below. She thought about this with seriousness in her heart, gripping, facing, and leaning into the walls.

Far down Highway 201, at its end, was a conglomeration of streetlights tipping in the wind; a hotel across the intersection; a closed Papa John's Pizzeria, Pizza Hut, Taco Bell, Dunkin Donuts, and finer restaurants up the way; a McDonalds on the nearest corner; and, past the glow of the streetlights, the dead Oakdale Mall. As Embree neared the glow, a box truck sped past the middle-of-night red light.

Starving, Embree stopped at the McDonalds drive through and spoke into the intercom, ordering from the all-day breakfast menu.

"What's up?" a voice said.

"Yeah, I'll have five Egg McMuffins, please," Embree said.

"First window, please."

Embree took out the last of her money and breathed deep, holding her hand to her face and scuffing around the corner to the sliding window, where a teenager from the projects greeted her.

"You're...standing there?" the man asked, confused.

"Well, duh," Embree said back.

"You could've gone inside, girl," he said.

"Just give me my fucking McMuffins," Embree said, slapping the money on the counter.

The man handed Embree a hefty bag of sandwiches, a few bills, a few coins, and a receipt.

"Good luck," he said, watching her walk away.

In the McDonald's back parking lot, Embree stuffed her face, forcing all five sandwiches into her gut without a drink in three minutes. The final two were so dry that she almost choked. The grease and salt of the ham and light sweetness of the English muffin were all delicious, she thought in so many words. When she was finished, she found her stomach aching.

Out of curiosity and with nothing better to do with what she was certain would be the end of her life, Embree hiked across the empty intersection past Keybank on the corner to the dead mall. The lot was wide, with the paint of the parking slots weathering away under a blanket of unkempt snow. The snowed-over dividing berms held a few dead pine shrubs and weed tufts.

Dragging her feet, Embree approached the southern storefront, which was laid with tall concrete slabs and had a harbor where the swinging doors stood, locked tight and smothered from the inside with yellow tarp and a sign that read "this store is now closed" with a street address directing to Scranton, a phone number, a website address, and in tall Roman lettering the name "Macy's." She followed the contour of the mall around, climbing and slipping up a culvert through the scrub and evergreens and wintering ash trees, over a guard rail and to a sidewalk. The storefronts above were laid of what seemed to be small yellowing bricks in the faded light of Johnson City and the moonlight. She spotted a footprint in the concrete of the sidewalk, passing the vast edge of pine scrub and leafless gingko trees and railings to closed-off entryways. She found it all so unremarkable.

Embree finally found the smashed glass of an entrance past The Bon-Ton, which she saw with its unlit lettering styled high along the store. The black plastic cordoning off the glass was torn open, and she hunched over and stepped through into a freezing, coal-black corridor. She set everything she owned on the tiling except for the knife and grill lighter, holding one in each hand. She lit the lighter in spurts, seeing the fanning glow ahead and all the filth and clusters of mouse shit upon the floor. Her staccato steps crushed the loose glass. She passed an oak bench; a row of fading-blue toddler's carts; an emptied-out coke machine; and, in the flame like a red dawn, Vinny in his closeness, dripping and drooling a black puke before disappearing. She cringed, knowing Vinny was an asshole, focusing on breathing softly and taking steps slowly.

Embree turned right into a tight hallway scribbled with graffiti. At the end was the locked glass door to an office and two doors to men's and women's restrooms. Inside, she drew a miserable emoji with an index finger on the mirror, around handprints, with its frown and triple bags under the eyes. She discovered that soap dispensers were dry, faucets handles were creaky, toilets were smeared with shit, and a urinal cradled a moldy and melting-out sandwich.

"How did that get there?" Embree thought. "Fuck, this place reeks."

Back in the main strip, Embree wandered, thumbing the lighter on and off, until she met the grand collection of benches and dead potted plants beneath the domed paneling of a snow-covered sky roof. A quiet, hoarse voice emerged from the shadows.

"Have you ever lived under the 201?" said the woman, almost whispering.

Embree drew closer with her knife ahead of her until she could see an old, pale-skinned, chubby Native American lady—until warming the woman's pitted face and all her wrinkles with the small aura of the grill lighter—and the woman stared and smiled, sharing her yellowed teeth.

"It's okay. I won't hurt you," said the woman. "I couldn't even if I wanted to. I'm disabled."

"Well, that's reassuring," Embree said. "Why are you here?"

"The same reason you are: rejected by society, abandoned by those you loved. Have you ever lived under the bridge?"

"No, but close to there," Embree said, welling up and confused.

"You have struggled," the woman said.

"Thanks, Nostradamus."

"And you will struggle much more," she said ominously. "But you will come out a strong, legendary woman."

"Now let me stop you right there," Embree laughed. "See, this here," she said, pointing to the watch she never owned. "This, here, is my death week. I'm finished. I fucking give up. I have nowhere to go and absolutely nobody to trust, nothing to eat or drink, nothing, nobody, zilch..."

"You will find your way," said the woman.

"The fuck is so special about that bridge, anyway?" Embree spat.

"The otters—everyone needs something to love."

"Otters?" Embree asked. "There's no fuckin otters around here. Just when I thought you were making sense, that you had some shred of hope to share, you fucking loon—you start to make me look normal," and, with that note, Embree blew out the flame theatrically and twisted around and vanished into the blackness.

PART 4

19

The snow blew across in sheets the day Embree crouched back through the broken glass of the condemned mall. She stepped through windblown snowdrifts, feeling the powder collect in her cuffs, melt, and refreeze inside the denim as she hiked. Staring aimlessly and lost in the eyes, she followed the curb of Reynolds Road uphill—gear in hand, the world nothing more than a downtrodden desert, and the tears and gunk of her blue eyes crusted over—and she cut left into the valley of Overbrook Road, and, at the road's lowest point, she spied the dam wall of Overbrook Reservoir, shuffling right onto Nelson Road and following it past all the neatly spaced townhouses to its end where the dam towered beyond gusts of snow and into the drab overcast.

"This is where I die," Embree mumbled.

Exhausted, Embree attempted to climb the slushed-over trail of the steep dam, slipping and falling hard several times onto her chest and face, the snow slipping under her sweatshirts and biting. She crawled up the final stretch to the crown, leaving prints of her clenched fists and pole and knife and lighter in the snow, with the duffel bag still strapped over her shoulder.

"What do I need this heavy shit for to die?" Embree thought, dropping her gear.

Embree slid down the hill to the concrete spillway of the reservoir, which was shaped like a puzzle piece and stretched far into the distance, with its wooded bluff shorelines to the far right and left all dead and vacant. A sign stood proudly in the snow: "New York flood control reservoir. Hours 6am to 6pm. No water or ice activities anytime."

Embree rolled her tired eyes and advanced onto the snowy ice empty-handed and cold, thinking what she guessed would be her final thoughts.

"If I fall through the ice, I'll drown," Embree said, assuring herself.

Embree wandered, zigzagging out to roughly the reservoir's middle where she jumped and stomped, trying to break through, but the ice didn't give. Sighing and then sobbing, she laid into the blanketing snow, feeling against her scalp the ice press back hard underneath, and she shut her eyes for the final time. The snow squall cooled her face until the flakes stuck, piling.

"My heat will melt some of the ice," Embree thought, "and the world's coldness will freeze it back around me. I'll be a relic until spring, and if they find me they'll wonder how I got here."

By noon, Embree was shivering and squinting beneath a thin layer of snow on her eyelids, cheeks, neck, fingers, and clothes, her toes and hands burning with what felt like a biting warmth, and she saw visions of her castle and of Jason joining her in her new life and protecting her, summer everlasting.

"Soon," Embree thought.

In the pitter-patter of falling snow, Embree heard the saving grace and quiet curse of footsteps. She wiped the snowflakes from her face with her numbing hand and glanced through the white brightness at the blurred man approaching at a jog, the mountainous silhouette of his ice fishing sled left far behind with its collapsed tent, jig and bait containers, and ice rods poking out to the side.

"Are you alright?" the man asked in a smooth voice.

"Huh?"

"What're you doing out here? Chilling?"

Embree smiled ever so gently back, delirious—her eyes like little slits.

Embree felt her nose running and saw the man standing in his glory—his jawline beard-studded with fine reddish-black hairs, his face twisted with concern, and his hands out of pocket and waiting to act. He wore boots and a black fleece over coveralls, his face bare and youthful and handsome against the flurries, with his hair black, short, and tousled and his eyes a deep green.

"You're shivering?" said the man.

"I'll b-be gone s-s-soon," Embree whispered.

"How in the Hell did you get here," he thought, eyeing the lumps of her hair, breasts, and shoes all mummified in snow, pausing and parting at the lips.

"I'm Luke. Umm, wait here I guess?" he said, running back to his sled.

Luke hunched over his sled, unstrapping the bungee cords, and he rushed back while holding a collapsed ice fishing tent and portable heater under his arms.

"Who are you?" Luke asked, plowing swathes of ice bare around Embree with his boots.

"Embree," she muttered. "Are you an angel?"

"Yes, beautiful, I'm here to save you. Sit up."

"Please, don't call me beautiful," Embree whispered, mouthing the words.

Luke unstrapped and unfolded the ice tent, popping open its spring-loaded limbs that drew out with the weatherproof fabric like a bat's wing, and he lifted and carefully placed the tent over Embree, who'd sat up and stooped over forward under her own weight and the heft of her confusion, and he moored the tent to the ice with custom corkscrews, working fast and unzipping the tent and reaching in for the heater after, flicking it on.

"Here, please, sit on the heater for now. Your hands are turning blue," Luke said, and after she wormed her way up, stumbling and breathing hard, the heater hissed past her pants and dangling fingers a slow heat.

Luke zipped up the tent and talked to her from the outside, squatting.

"Are you okay in there?"

"Y-yes."

"What were you thinking? You wanted to die the most painful way possible?"

"Luke, r-right? There is no p-p-pain like the p-pain of my past."

Luke raised his eyebrows. Embree smelled the rot of her wet shoes as the heater billowed and air circulated, and she started to feel her legs and hands itch first a little, then terribly, and scratched at them, starting to cry again silently, herself a ghost to him resurrecting.

Luke crouched with his hands folded, waiting patiently for most of ten minutes before speaking up again, calculating his words for fear of losing her before they even started.

"Are you warming up, Embree? You're okay, right? You have a friend now."

"Thanks, Luke," she said, beginning to sob, with the tent fabric muffling her words.

Luke took this reassuringly and waited again for minutes, racking his fingers—the snow squalling once more and pelting the tent and the canvas of his coveralls and face.

"Are you still cold?"

"Ya-y-yes."

"Fuck this, then—can we go somewhere and get warm?"

Silence reigned for a minute and, fearing rejection, this weighed upon Luke's mind and heart.

"Please, can we go get warm?" Luke begged, mostly for her sake.

"I d-don't even know you," Embree said softly. "How d-do I know you're not here to h-hurt me?"

"If I wanted to hurt you, I'd have let you freeze," Luke said back, his voice rich and deep and soothing like the countryside breeze. "Come on, let's get out of here."

"How are y-you even here anyway? You c-can't ice fish here."

"Fuck that sign," Luke said.

Embree smirked, mustering up her strength and sitting upright and feeling a warmth pump from her heart for the sake of his rebellion—a lawlessness not unlike Jason's—and again her thoughts became like cards being shuffled, and the only thought she could grip onto in the lunacy was that of cathartic risk-taking, overlooking her recent traumas.

"Hey, let's get out of here," Luke insisted.

20

Along the crest of the dam, Luke dragged his packed sled by its rope in one hand and held leaning, stumbling, shivering, and frail Embree by the shoulder with the other. Fading in and out and in the delicate tapping of the snowstorm, she could feel beneath his coveralls the bulk and curves of his forearms—a true fisherman's quality, she thought—and, in their hiking, she could feel through the bridge of their arms their hearts intertwine.

Parked on the roadside—what wasn't there before—was an ocean-blue Subaru WRX, and Luke carried the weight of her leaning carcass down the winding trail, around old barbed wire, and back to Nelson Road. He unlocked and opened the car door for her, leading her gently and low into the belly of the car and its leather seat, and he left his gear outside, jogged to the driver's side and opened his door, pressed the starter button, and immediately cranked the heat to high for her.

"Just leave me outside. I'm going to stink up your nice car," Embree said.

"No, never," Luke said back. "You're safe now."

Embree melted into the seat, comfortable yet ringing in confusion, blushing along blued cheeks.

"How about a hot shower?"

"That would be so nice of you, but seriously, you have to let me go," Embree muttered back.

"Come on, Embree. Things will get better. I promise."

"But I don't even know you, though," Embree said, coughing out the last word into her reddening hand.

"You have to let someone in for a moment to get to

know them, so how about you get to know me, then? Just give me a small chance. Want to get dinner later? What's your favorite?"

"I want a macaroni chili bowl, and I don't want to ever be touched again," Embree said, shivering and reminiscing.

"Okay," Luke said, smiling. "That sounds good to me."

Luke drove smoothly but aggressively—California stops. He took Embree down Oakdale Road; the mountainous slopes and twists of East Maine Road, past the fire station trooper trap and a piebald mountain range vista; and lastly through the four-way intersection of death with its yellow-blinking streetlights overhead, by the lonely Mirabito, onto Ames Road, along which he turned sharply toward a cottage alongside Nanticoke Creek that skirted all the shimmering-white farmland that touched distant Route 26.

The cottage was a generous gift from Luke's uncle, who had died from the stubbornness of waiting out treatable cancer. The cottage was made from jade-green wooden slat siding and flagstone shingles, with three burgundy framed windows and a door hung along its one-story base. Moss overlapped parts of the curved, snow-shoveled sidewalk leading aside from a stone driveway. One old walnut tree creaked beside the cottage, towering before the wood fence that charted the yard's edge, and still the gleaming flurries collected. Embree soaked it all in, hugging her knees and crouching into herself, while Luke revved his car atop the driveway.

"I know it's nothing great, but this is my home," Luke said.

"I think it's lovely."

"You're welcome to anything I own in there, of course. Take your time."

Embree escaped the car in its heated-seat grandeur and beelined for the door, crossing her forearms and burying her hands in her armpits for heat. Luke jogged up behind her and past her, grinding the key through the bolt lock fast, swinging the door open, and throwing her a hopeful grin.

Inside were six small rooms—foyer, den, kitchen, bedroom, bathroom, and basement—all open to one another. The foyer was constructed of off-white walls and slate stone floor, with a half-loaded coat and boot closet to the right, blossoming into the den, which they stepped into swiftly, leaving their shoes on. Embree first spotted in the den the eight-point and nine-point bucks on the wall above either armrest of the couch, stately, with one wearing an orange hunter's hat. Then she saw the plasma television across from her and gun cases beside a back window displaying the panorama of an iced-over creek and an oak table before the couch with an ashtray, cameras, and other filmmaking equipment scattered across its top.

"You're a filmmaker?" Embree asked, still clutching herself.

"Here, let's get you warm. We can talk about it after."

Luke led Embree past the oak railing separating the rooms and past the neatness of the kitchenware, coffee pot, sink basin, cabinets, and two empty bottles of beer along the open and clean kitchen countertop, holding his hand out in view of the bathroom before opening and reaching into a closet for a towel, handing it to her.

"Please, take a hot shower. Take as long as you need."

"Thank you," she said back. "But I've got no fresh

clothes. I have nothing."

"I'll find you something while you're in there, or we can just wash what you're wearing after you're done."

"Yeah, that," Embree said back softly.

Embree closed and locked the bathroom door behind her. The bathroom was tight with a an off-white toilet; one-piece sink, oak cabinet, and mirror; green tiling; and a shower with white porcelain tub and a curtain adorned with drawings of hooked trout jumping from the water. She opened the mirror cabinet, eyeing and taking out his triple-blade razor and spying a pill bottle labeled with "lurasidone," "8omg tablet," and "Luke Bronson." She closed the swinging mirror until it snapped, and she stripped down, shedding the outermost layers with ease and then tearing the innermost shirt and her panties from the clotted blood and crud of her body, suffering waves of chills and gooseflesh.

In the shower, Embree's skin stung against the hot shotgun flow, and filth flowed from her skin in streamlets and flushed as grayish-black soot into the drain. She simply stood in the flow for fifteen minutes, twisting—the bones of her legs and hands seemingly an everlasting wick for coldness—until she could begin to feel the creeping warmth inside her skeleton. She raked her fingers through her matted, knotted brunette locks, and bits of leaves and black specks of bark fell free. She shampooed her hair twice, and she could feel it twisting back into its naturally frayed waves. She considered shaving the hair of her legs, armpits, and groin, but in her cacophony of thoughts she figured the hair could be a shield against Luke's possible advance, and still she soaked in the warmth. She stretched like a leopard and almost slipped on the wet tiling and then tied the towel around her breasts and waist, tousling her fresh hair and feeling her mood freshen as well, skyrocketing unreasonably and inviting rash decision-making once again. She opened the door just a crack at first.

"Luke?" Embree probed.

"Hey, you alright? I'm on the sofa," Luke hollered back.

Embree stepped into view and struck a facetious sexy pose, holding her hand to her head and popping out the curves of her towel-wrapped waist and smiling.

"Thanks again."

"Wow! You look—umm—you clean up really nice?" Luke said, tongue-tied.

"Thanks for not calling me beautiful," Embree said earnestly, pondering and starting to cry again. "But I don't care anymore. You can call me whatever you like."

"What's wrong?"

"I was supposed to die today. La tristesse dura toujours."

"Only if you let it," Luke said back immediately.

Embree stood perplexed, sniveling, and red-faced. Luke wasn't supposed to know what she said, she thought, but somehow he did.

"I hope you will never have to understand," she said.

Luke laid into the cushions, stoic and patient, and he raised his eyebrows again.

"Would you like to see my work?"

"Yes, please," Embree replied.

Luke rose and escorted Embree just beyond the bathroom to his bedroom, the bed of which was sheeted in Canadian hunting scenery with its moose, undergrowth, caribou, and lichens, and from the wall hung a full black bear skin, an eleven-point whitetail's head staring left, and a semiautomatic jet-black bullpup rifle hung by a nail through the trigger guard. A cedar desk with more filmmaking equipment and a computer stood in the corner. Embree adored it all, mesmerized.

"What's that on the wall?" Embree asked, pointing to a glass-framed silver rectangle engraved with a sideways triangle.

"That's my silver play button. You earn one for hitting 100,000 subscribers. I'm an outdoors YouTuber."

"Holy shit. That's amazing. I never even thought about doing that, wow. How many do you have?"

"Thanks—I'm up to 189,000, give or take a little. I think I'm the biggest outdoors YouTuber in New York, at least from what I've seen. The revenue is steady, but the rise in subscribers has slowed down. I don't think that I'll ever hit the gold play button, at least not before I'm fifty, if YouTube even still exists by then."

"What's the gold play button?"

"You get it for hitting 1,000,000 subscribers on YouTube. It's the dream. Assuming five times the revenue along with it—we could travel anywhere."

"We?" Embree asked, raising an eyebrow, still towel-wrapped.

"Yes, we—if you'd want. I don't know what it is, but I like you. Please stick around."

"I'm flattered, but there's some things you should know about me before you go picking the rotten apple out of the bin."

"Like what?"

"Like, I know Vinny is looming over you as we speak."

"May I ask: who is Vinny?"

"He's an asshole."

"You're not making any sense."

"I see demons. I hear screaming. I get pissed off, forgetful, depressed, and so many other things that have taken me too long to realize aren't normal."

"You have hallucinations?"

"How are you supposed to understand it's not normal when it's all you've ever known?" Embree cried.

"I get it; trust me, I do, and I don't think any less of you for it."

Embree paused and then laid into him with an unexpected hug, overlying her calloused hands and squeezing him hard enough where her breasts flattened out against the towel.

"Save me, please—or else kill me."

"Do you want real help?"

"I don't know anymore."

"Here," Luke said softly, "let me make a phone call. I'll go throw your clothes in the washer downstairs while I take care of the call, okay?"

Embree waited on the couch, still suffering waves of chills across her skin—but not from the remnant winter's fangs in her bones; rather, she got chills from the shock of it all and from experiencing a kindness and altruistic care for once, just once, that rivaled Jason's.

The view of Nanticoke creek was incredible, Embree thought, as a buck mink hopped and pirouetted along the far bank, twisting into muskrat holes and popping back out. She liked the hunting shows playing on the television, too, and she leaned back hard into the cushion, her belly bent and taut skin rippled into itself. For twenty minutes, she watched the man on the television hunt a big atypical buck over food plots before Luke returned, stomping up the stairs.

"I got you an appointment. Trust me, it sucks but it will help you so much in the end."

"With who?"

"The best psychiatrist in the area."

"Luke, I can't afford that," Embree said.

"Don't worry. I can."

"Out of pocket?"

"Yes."

"I don't know how I feel about this. What's his name?"

"My psychiatrist, Dr. Noham—she's a her."

"Your psychiatrist?"

"Yes."

"Oh, I'm so sorry for what I said earlier."

"It's okay. I totally understand."

"What's wrong with you? Or, umm, sorry, I don't mean it in a bad way...but, what's..."

"I have schizophrenia," Luke interrupted, "and OCD, bad."

"What, like, do you feel—the symptoms, I guess?"

Luke fell into the couch two cushions down from Embree, treading lightly and guessing that he should give her the space she often needed.

"I don't really like to talk about it," he sighed, pausing. "I don't want to scare you off."

"Honestly...I don't think that's possible."

"How about the schizophrenia now and we save the OCD for some other time?" Luke asked.

"Okay."

"Well," Luke paused. "It's kind of hard to describe. I get hallucinations and delusions, of course—auditory hallucinations, persecutory delusions."

"So do I! I think?"

"But there's more to it than that. There's a part called flat affect. Back before I got help, I would become stuck, and I wouldn't be able to show emotion, and sometimes I'd sit there and say the same shit over and over again and wouldn't react to people, they told me. I was trapped in my own mind. I'm not perfect still, either. It still takes hold of me once in a while."

"Wow," Embree said. "Want to be crazy together?"

"We'll be unstoppable," Luke said, smirking back.

21

Embree scarfed down two macaroni chili bowls and a house burger at Food and Fire that evening in Johnson City, dining with Luke, himself like a stone against all the rumbling footsteps and conversation around. The tables were wooden and the air smelled of various barbeques. They chatted earlier on the sofa about hunting and fishing, their successes, their interests, their near misses, their work, and how it's all affected them. In doing so, talking of their overlying dreams and desires, their souls melted together, still strangers but their bodies moving closer together on the couch.

"Luke, this chili is the best thing I've ever tasted—thanks so much."

"You don't have to thank me every time we get something together, you know."

"Luke, the creamy macaroni, the chili, all mixed together!"

"I know, girl; it's great."

Luke ordered another water and took the straw, still tipped with paper, out and blew through it such that the paper shot toward Embree's neck, and she held back a laugh due to her full mouth.

"So, are we, like, dating?" Embree whispered.

"Well, I mean, isn't this a date? Seems kinda like a date to me. Of course, it's up to you."

"I dig it," Embree said, smiling back. "I just met you this morning, and this is all so crazy, but yeah—maybe, just maybe—I think I'm starting to believe in love at first sight."

"Okay, then, I gotta think up a cute nickname for you,"

Luke said, jesting.

Embree's belly was hard with food, aching and distended ever so slightly by the meal's end; however, having learned the value of food, she made sure to finish her burger and fries.

That night Embree slept on the sofa, insistent that she take the sofa and Luke take the bed, though Luke wanted it the other way around, eventually conceding to her stubbornness. The sofa was soft and fresh with febreze and far more comfortable than anything the pinched nerve in her back had laid into in months. She experienced lucid night terrors and, despite having some control, woke in a fury and fell off the sofa from screaming Clicky hurling himself at her mind's eye. She only slept two hours, watching television and pacing about the den in circles the rest of the night.

"Morning, Bubs," Luke chuckled, eyeing her standing there in Camila's sweatshirt and jeans all cleaned. "Coffee, toast, eggs, venison?"

"Yes, please, all of it, Bubs."

"How would you like everything?"

"I'd be more than happy with having them however you like yours."

Luke fried the eggs sunny side up, cooked the chilled venison from the refrigerator with butter a sizzling blue rare, brewed the coffee black, and prepared the toast a light brown on the same skillet as the eggs, forking more than half onto Embree's plate after fifteen minutes at the stove. They dined on the sofa, Luke in his t-shirt and checkered boxers, his legs thick with black hair and toned, and with Embree still in her comfy clothes.

Finished, Luke took their plates to the sink, and with

Luke sitting back down, Embree leaned over and hugged him and laid into his cheek with a long, soft kiss. She could feel the warmth flowing from her heart and his cheek warming, too. Nobody spoke; it was a tender moment amidst a very hard winter.

"You're too cool, Bubs. I've never seen something so lovely so close to death, and I'm a professional killer trained in hunting nature's loveliest."

She paced after scraping her plate clean, etching around the walls and furniture of the den with her steps and eyeing all the rifles, shotguns, and the wicked spiderwebbing frame of a crossbow in the gun cases—some vintage and others used.

"I'm glad you can see through my tears."

Over five days they had taken it easy, at Embree's request, holding a bonfire outside Luke's cottage between the two of them and sharing stories of their struggles—her homelessness, his catatonia—and how they ultimately came to be and what they could do together for fun; also, going mudding through the frozen-over slop down the winding, dipping trail of Griffin park to the mouth of Nanticoke creek and back several times over in the Subaru; and finally watching television and relaxing and, toward the end of the week, making out with a softness and tongue twisting that challenged everything she'd ever felt and known.

D-Day arrived in a hurry, Embree thought. Luke dressed in his best flannel shirt and jeans. She filled three blank sheets of paper front and back with notes about her symptoms or whatever she thought may be wrong in her life, scribbling in rambling, stringy sentences and short, bulleted words: "Clicky," "Vinny," "concentration," "rapes," "death," "screaming," "hyperactivity," "repeating myself," "sleep issues," "persecution," "irritability," "suicidal ideation," "paranoia," "risks," "crying," "anxiety," "guilt," "mood swings," "apathy," "weight loss," and all strung out in so many stories and words as she tried hard to remember over hours every crumb. Luke loomed from a distance, careful to give her privacy despite hearing about all but the rapes.

"Do you want me to come in with you, to your appointment, or do you want me to wait in the lobby?"

"Ummm," she said, "how about I'll come out for you when I'm ready?"

"Whatever you want, Bubs. But let's get going. The doctor likes us to be on time."

They sped through the noontime snow and slush of the freshly salted roads to a complex in Endwell, the neighborhood near Murphy's Island, along the back road of Picken Street. Embree, recognizing the blinking caution lights guarding River Road, was amazed at what was under her nose the whole time—that is, if, as she hoped, this venture was actually all it was cracked up to be.

They trotted through the blanketing snow up the staircase and through two doors where the lobby laid. Embree was hopeful, but, deep down and without Luke knowing, truly she also wagered that all of this was futile and a joke. Stress welled up heavily in her chest as she scoped out the lobby—a Picasso-style artwork of African and European faces behind a thin waterfall to the left, a hallway labeled "Dr. Noham" just beyond the painting, what seemed to be speech and other therapists' rooms down the hall and perhaps up the stairs, orderly leather sofas and basket-mesh foot rests, a tea and water and magazine station in the corner, and a vacant and dark glass booth hub up ahead. They waited, cradled by the sofas for just a few minutes.

A striking, young-looking Indian lady rounded the corner, wearing a tan skirt and clacking heels and girdled by a thick black belt, waving.

"Embree?" Dr. Noham inquired.

Embree sighed, rising and shuffling into the hallway as Dr. Noham doubled back, with Luke still patiently sitting on the sofa.

Inside Dr. Noham's office hung gorgeous, painterly collages from all the walls and stood a pearl-white sofa; a recliner across from the sofa; a desk; and a maple stand with a smart phone, tablet, and copy of the DSM-5.

"Hi, Embree, I'm Dr. Noham. Please, take a seat. Luke tells me you're struggling. Is that true, dear? What are you experiencing?"

Embree didn't speak; she slowly, silently handed over her three sheets of paper, with tears beginning to collect in the bottom of her eyes and her face reddening. She regretted writing about the rapes, however brief, but it was too late to take it back.

"Dear God, all this?" Dr. Noham asked, scanning fast and flipping again and again until she'd read each side of sheet twice, disturbed.

"Umm, I'm Embree. I was in the hospital once. The doctor there said I had mild bipolar," she said, pausing. "It was involuntary admission, and I wasn't there long."

"You're kidding me," Dr. Noham said, still flipping the sheets. "That's really what the doctor said? What did she start you on?"

"Lithium."

"Just lithium?"

"Yes."

"That's ridiculous. Okay, so, Clicky and Vinny—these are visual hallucinations?"

"Mostly yes—I mean, I hear them too sometimes, and then there's the screaming, the loud, horrifying, godforsaken screaming."

Embree noticed diplomas from New York University and a residency at Brown University displayed along the left wall.

"Okay, so, first of all, you should be on an antipsychotic immediately. That doctor is out of her mind. There's nothing mild about what you've been through."

"So it's severe?"

"Uhh, yes! Truthfully, I've never seen this before."

Embree felt a warmth and vindication in her heart above her shaking knees and jaw and tapping feet.

"What do you mean?"

"Your case—I've never seen one quite like this. I don't look it, I know, but I'm fifty years old. I've been doing this for twenty years."

"What's so special about my case?"

"Well, do you know how bipolar works?"

"They ran me through it at the hospital."

"Okay, so you're cycling through mania and depression several times a week or experiencing them at the same time sometimes? That is, you're experiencing symptoms of both in quick succession or on top of each other?"

"Yes, I suppose"

"That's what's known as a bipolar mixed state. It comes with the highest risk for suicide out of all states of mood illness. Are you feeling suicidal right now?"

"No—yes, I mean, kind of, always."

"Do you have a plan?"

"I don't know. I just kind of think about hurting myself with whatever is around me."

"And what would that be?"

"Usually something involving knives, bridges, drowning, or freezing."

"But you aren't actively planning to kill yourself at the moment?"

"No, I guess not. What's wrong with me?"

"There's nothing wrong with you. You're one of the strongest women I've ever met—you were molested as a child from some sick piano teacher and more recently raped, twice?! Unfortunately, you're ill, but we can work on that. Bipolar patients commonly are able to stabilize and eventually lead relatively normal, healthy lives; there is hope. Okay, so, Embree, do these hallucinations happen at the same time as your mood episodes—your depression and mania?"

"Sometimes yes, sometimes no."

"Well, here's the deal. You likely have PTSD from the rapes and maybe even Jason's death—all of which I'm so sorry about, truly—but the other diagnosis is more complicated than simply 'bipolar.' Here, I like showing people this."

Dr. Noham flipped to a blank sheet of paper on her clipboard, drawing lines with triangular spikes and lines of scribbling fuzziness separately, and then she drew a third line combining the forms into one disorganized, overlapping mess.

"This line represents every form of bipolar, types one

through four," Dr. Noham said, pointing to the triangles. "The ups and downs—mania and depression—typify this mood disorder. The line with scribbles represents recurring periods of schizophrenia—hallucinations, delusions, flat affect, and more—of which you only need so many symptoms to be diagnosed. Now, bipolar one includes hallucinations and delusions, but they are always mood-concurrent; that is, they happen at the same time as the mania or depression. If your hallucinations and delusions continue outside your mood episodes, you have the gray area between schizophrenia and bipolar or what's known as schizoaffective."

"So what's my diagnosis exactly?"

"I would say, for now, knowing what I know so far, that it's schizoaffective, bipolar type, mixed state along with PTSD."

"What do I do about this?"

Embree was trembling violently at this point, like never before, at the knees and hands and stuttering her words.

"Are you able to stop shaking?"

"I don't know," Embree said. "This doesn't usually happen."

"White coat syndrome," Dr. Noham chuckled. "You might have a problem with anxiety, too. But, anyway, treatment can be a hard process of trial and error, and with most any medicine there are consequences and side effects. I think we should start you off with lithium, valproic acid, and aripiprazole. They should have had you on an antipsychotic, like aripiprazole, from the start."

"What are the side effects for those?"

"Lithium and valproic acid require blood tests because

they have a narrow therapeutic range—that is, to say, they can damage the liver if too concentrated and not be effective if not concentrated enough. That's the main concern."

Dr. Noham took out her tablet, touching all over the screen and talking through the motions fast.

"All three at once?" Embree asked.

"Yes, that's what they should have tried in the first place, I think. Aripiprazole can cause difficulty speaking, restlessness, drooling, stiffness, and uncontrolled movements commonly; uncommonly, blurred vision, headaches, eyelid spasms, trouble breathing, increased heart rate, and nervousness; and, rarely, it can cause convulsions, blood pressure changes, high fever, sweating, lip smacking, urinary deficiency, muscle spasms, loss of consciousness, and severe tiredness and muscle stiffness. If any of these happen," Dr. Noham added, handing her a business card, "especially the rare side effects, please call me on my main line, and if you're ever in trouble—suicidal or otherwise and just need to talk—please call my emergency number, okay?"

"Okay, but that's a ridiculous list of side effects," Embree said. "God help me."

"You'll be okay, dear. You're safe now, and it may be hard, but we'll figure this out. You won't believe what's ahead of you—something like you've never experienced. Now, which pharmacy would you like to pick up your medicine at?"

"Luke told me that we'll go to CVS on North Street, I guess, please."

Dr. Noham fiddled with her tablet and then stood up, stately.

"I'll work on setting you up with a great therapist, if that's okay with you. She'll help, especially with the PTSD. How about we meet again in two weeks?"

"Yes, please and thank you."

Dr. Noham walked through the door, motioning Embree into a room alongside with desks, tables, a computer, credit card machine, sample packs of medicine stacked into an open cabinet, a printer and fax machine, and some of her lunch of fruit and sandwiches packed neatly off to the side in Tupperware. A balding, happy man sat in the seat by the computer.

"This is my husband, Brian. He takes care of the billing. It was great meeting you, Embree. Please, take care, and don't hesitate to call."

"I'm sorry; I have to go get Luke," Embree said. "I'm broke."

"Okay, no problem," Brian said back.

Luke walked through the doorway and paid with a black Visa the first visit of many, already having met his deductible for the year.

"Productive session?" Luke asked.

22

That evening, Luke looked through the kitchen window at the meadow across the street with its striking, snow-covered ant hills like little Kilimanjaros and how the sun set in smiles on their sides. He was washing dishes. D-Day would come over and over, Embree knew, and in different forms, and now it was time to take medicine and cross fingers.

"Luke, can you help me open these?"

"Here," Luke said, twisting and picking at the plastic wrappers. "I got something for you."

In the CVS bag holding Embree's medicines, Luke mined out a pill container labeled by the weekdays, smiling.

"Don't smirk at me. That's a shitty present."

"Whoa, okay there, Bubs, chill."

"Don't tell me what to do. I'll fucking kill you."

"Please chill?"

Embree stayed silent, crossing her arms. Luke walked aside and distributed lithium, valproic acid, and aripiprazole into every weekday slot save for this day, which he handed over to her in a clenched palm.

"Cheers," Luke said, trying to reach her and handing her some water, too.

"Nothing about this is funny. The fuck am I supposed to do about this?"

"About what?"

"All these side effects."

"Bubs, look, this is what the doctor told me at first, and this is just how it has to go: you try a medicine, see if it works, then keep trying medicines until you find the right combination. It's a process. She has to ease you out of this. She once said to me: 'the longer you've been sick, the worse the case generally is.'"

"I've been ill most of my life, maybe all of it."

"Well, don't expect this to be easy then, but I know you can do it. There's no pain like the pain of your past, remember?"

Embree nodded, tipping back her head and chugging the pills with water, struggling to swallow them.

"How many medicines did you have to try?"

"Three."

The following day, Embree woke in a dizzying rush, exploding from the couch, and she heard Luke rummaging in his room, so she slinked over for a look. He was arranging cameras and chest mounts and fishing containers in a backpack. He strolled over to the refrigerator, opening it and grabbing four little containers of spikes and mousies.

"I'm filming today, Bubs, for the channel. Want to come?"

"Okay," Embree said, more for Luke than herself, swirling in a stew of tiredness and depression.

Luke arranged his auger, tent, ice rods, backpack, shovel, cascaded buckets, and flasher in the sled atop the back seat of the car, strapping it all in with bungee cords. Embree took the front seat, not buckling and leaning her seat back for a nap as far as it would go against the ice fishing equipment.

"Careful of the rods, honey."

Embree stared back murderously.

"Please?" Luke said, smiling. "Come on, we're gonna

have a good time. I don't go fishing; I go catching."

The roads were shingled with spots of black ice and snowdrifts, and through the twists and turns of wooded back roads, Luke felt the tires of his car slip on several occasions, despite its four-wheel drive. Embree fell back asleep almost upright in her seat, snoring, her head folded into her shoulder like a poisonous, fading flower.

Luke passed barns, fenced pastures, and farmland and parked on the shoulder of the road in a shallow snowdrift by a willow thicket. A snowed-over log blocked the tractor-wide trail leading two hundred feet down, across knolls, to Ford Pond, a private pond that Luke had asked permission from the farmer's family to fish.

"Bubs, we're here," Luke said, touching her shoulder.

Embree woke, gasping.

"Please, for the love of God, don't touch me there."

Luke was confused as to what she meant as he'd been holding her by the shoulder and the small of her back every time they'd softly make out, but he accepted her words nonetheless and drew back his hand.

They exited the car and Luke opened the trunk by pressing his key fob.

"Here, Bubs, wear this. It'll keep you warm and it floats if you fall through," Luke said, holding up thick gray coverall ice bibs loaded with pockets, pull cords, and other accessories.

"You wear it. I'm not cold and I don't give a shit if I fall through," Embree said dimly.

"Okay," Luke said, tossing the bibs back in the trunk, sighing, and gently clicking it closed.

The march to the ice was nippy and foreboding, with flurries sailing into their faces in the blustery winds.

Embree squinted. Luke dragged the sled with its awful grinding as it dug down through the snow with its weight and touched the start of the ice. A rectangular ice skating rink had been fashioned to the side, bare and crisscross sliced, and he knew not to touch it per request of Mr. Ford. The pond was about six acres, edged by firs and frozen-over cattails to either side, and they trudged on a hundred yards to the center of its northern end.

Luke unstrapped the equipment and opened wide his backpack, pulling out the camera equipment and snapping together the chest mount across his muscled torso and withdrawing and locking the telescoping legs of a tripod and screwing another camera to its top.

"Gotta film the intro, Bubs. You in?"

"I'll stay behind you," she said, the best she could muster up.

Luke pressed the camera on.

"What's up, YouTube! Luke Bronson here, from L.B. Outdoors, here to smash the shit out of the panfish today! I have a special guest, my Bubs, Embree!" he exclaimed, aiming his thumb at her without breaking eye contact with the camera. "She's a great charter fisherwoman, and you'll be seeing a lot more of her in the future!"

Embree faked a smile and waved. Luke pressed the camera off.

"See, that easy, Bubs. Thousand dollar video in the making."

"What's the most you ever made from one video?"

"Ten grand. I was ice fishing the river for big pike a long time ago. That video put me on the map."

"Holy shit, okay, so what do I do now?"

"What's mine is yours, Bubs. Grab an ice rod and tip

the jig head with some mousies. Don't let the cup of mousies freeze, though—put them back in the backpack. I'll drill some holes."

Luke took the hand auger and drilled, grinding and plunking through the ice five holes in a line twenty feet apart from one another fast, kicking the slush and water aside from each with his boot and laying the auger down when he was done, taking care not to chip the blades. He took the flasher and uncoiled its sonar bell, flicking the flasher on and dropping the bell into each hole, and he observed the readout for fish—thin yellow-to-red lines on the circular LED screen between the blue line of ice and the green line of pond bottom.

"This hole, Bubs—there's something here; drop down. Have you ever used one of these?" Luke said, pointing to the flasher. "Here's bottom and your lure will be the thin line in-between along with any fish, and up here's the ice. First step is to locate the fish. Then we set up camp and go to town."

Embree squatted and opened her bail, letting line flow from the short rod, wiggling its sensitive tip as the tipped ice dot plummeted below.

"And, there, close your bail," Luke directed. "Now bring it up a little. You want to be above the fish, especially crappies. Mind if I film now?"

"No, go for it," Embree muttered, just going through the paces.

Luke positioned the tripod setup to the side and pressed it and his chest camera on, and both cameras bleeped and shone with a small red LED. He put his chest up to the flasher, where a thin green line turned yellow and then red, rising, until it met the thinnest red line of the jig and until, at the same moment, Embree's pole tip ticked down, and she ripped up into the fish, ever so slightly grinning and reeling in-between pumps of the rod.

"Embree's got the first fish of the day, folks! We're just locating them for now; when we find a good hole, we'll pop up the tent and break out the heater and snacks."

"Snacks?" Embree said, pumping.

"I always keep a secret compartment of snacks, Bubs," Luke smiled.

Embree pulled from the pulsating water a wriggling, eight inch, iridescent purple bluegill, which tossed itself about on the ice aimlessly as she shook the hook free from its jaw. She was fitted with three pound test on an ultralight ice rod—perfect for finicky clear-water panfish.

Luke moored the tent to the ice after clearing the blanketing snow with the shovel, screwing anchors into its side much like Embree once did with her tent. Inside the tent all, including themselves in their dim coloring, was dark except for the ice, which glowed a translucent blue, and the propane heater hissed in the corner like a talkative cobra.

Luke and Embree jigged side by side, sitting on flipped buckets with the tripod setup ahead of them, filming, creating a pile of bluegill and black-speckled crappie between them, and they took a few minutes to count their catch once they approached a limit of fifty bluegill each. They moved the tent to another hole where they fried banana slices atop an oiled cast-iron pan, which rested above a propane flame, all in view of the cameras, and finally they limited out on crappie at twenty five each three hours in. He talked about tips and techniques the whole time, filling the silence and explaining every element in a way that mesmerized her. At the finish, he held up his hand for a high five in view of the camera, and she obliged, albeit meekly and halfheartedly.

"That's an exceptional haul, Bubs! Now the work begins."

Luke laid out the panfish in tight rows until he had a massive sheet of their one hundred and fifty panfish, and he waved Embree in, talking to the camera.

"We slammed them today, folks. Embree, come on in, Bubs. This is your first bluegill and crappie limit, right?"

Embree nodded, squatting behind all the fish with her arms folded over her knees, smirking and silent. Luke took a video, gesturing with an upturned thumb, and framed the camera squarely at the fish to later make a high quality thumbnail. Then, he collapsed and strapped up the tent and took the shovel, scooping heaps of fish on film into the buckets like a janitor on payday, a classy gag.

"Bubs, do you want to take the sled for me? This has gotta be one hundred pounds of fish."

Later that night, after a spell of rest on the couch laying together and leaving the frozen fish inside to warm, Luke and Embree set up for filleting near the kitchen sink. They each had a bucket with their limits of bluegill and crappie— a total of seventy-five fish each—and, feeling confident, he was stupid enough to speak up.

"I bet you twenty bucks I finish first."

"Okay, you're on."

"Ready, go!"

Embree took her time eyeing and honing her fillet knife, finally digging in after Luke had already done two fish, filleting them the same way as striped bass and walleyes and most of the others. To her, it was a simple assignment. She finished filleting the panfish boneless ten minutes before Luke, an hour and twenty minutes in.

"Wow, Bubs, you smoked me. I knew I fucking loved you."

Embree curtsied facetiously with a straight face, her true colors suppressed.

"Come on, fork it over!"

Luke reached into his wallet and, grinning, pulled out a twenty dollar bill and handed it over, still filming.

"Okay, you can turn that fucking thing off now," Embree said, irritated.

Luke pressed the button. They were left with a mountain of fresh fillets—hundreds of dollars' worth.

At the end of the following week—Embree growing more tired by the day and taking her pills nightly—they visited Dr. Noham again, who welcomed Embree in.

"So, Embree, how are you doing?" Dr. Noham said, finding her seat.

"Tired, depressed, overwhelmed by boredom some-times."

"Are you still having hallucinations?"

Embree already was shaking at the knees and puckering her lips.

"Yes, and terrible night terrors: monsters hurling themselves at me or running through the dark, screaming. I wake up flying off the couch."

"I see. Are you feeling suicidal?"

"It depends on the day. Sometimes I have so much energy and I'm content and confused, but most of the time I'm so down and depressed."

"Do you have a plan?"

"Not really."

"How is your sleep?"

"I'm getting more and more tired. Every day I'm sleeping more. I slept most of last week on Luke's couch."

"Luke's a great guy, you know. He's been through a lot."

"I know."

"Embree, I think we should give the aripiprazole another two weeks to soak in and stay on the valproic acid and lithium for now. I might add benztropine for your shaking; it's an anti-Parkinsonian medication. I'll have you go in for blood work before we see each other next—in, say, two weeks again?"

"Okay, wonderful," Embree added. "Are we done? I need a nap."

23

The snow fell in timpani onto the European mount of a seven-by-eight elk Luke left hanging from the back of the cottage, above the back window. He'd harvested the elk on film four years ago with his father, a deathbed trip, before all the mourning and longing for more time.

Embree devolved over the next two weeks into a sluggish façade. It became difficult for her to walk any distance. She meandered down the stairs to help Luke by trying to do the laundry, and on her way back up, stumbling, she had to lie down at the crown of the stairs from exhaustion. Having slept for eighteen hours and with nothing perceivably left to do, she laid on the oak slats until he found her, panting and with her shoulder blades aching.

"Embree! Are you okay?"

"I—," Embree said, "I've never been okay. I need to get back on the couch."

Luke carried Embree like cordwood to the couch, setting her down gently.

"Do you want me to call the doctor?"

"No."

"What can I do to help?"

"Just turn on the TV, please, Bubs, and go have a good day filming."

"I'm not leaving you like this to suffer alone. We'll watch TV together."

Embree didn't watch the program, where they were slamming tuna commercially by jigging long Sabiki rigs, but rather she flickered at the eyelids and nodded off briefly almost twenty times before the program was over, collapsed into herself and sinking into the crack between cushions, with Luke just past her feet watching the show intently.

Fading, Embree took her aripiprazole, lithium, and valproic acid that night with contempt, and, truly, she only did it for Luke.

The next day, in the afternoon before her appointment, Embree and Luke visited the Binghamton zoo—wanting to do something, for once, low-key—spying all the monkeys, insects, sea life, dangerous game, pythons, and more. She lumbered at a pace one third of his, dying, and he stayed by her side, at times holding her hand.

That evening, Embree shuffled into the doctor's office, breathless, having slept another two weeks away for the most part, save for two days earlier in the week of overflowing excitement.

"Luke, come in with me, please," Embree said in the lobby, under her breath.

"How are you doing, dear?" Dr. Noham asked.

"She can barely talk," Luke said. "She's so exhausted."

"Your paintings?" Embree mumbled, folding into herself and pointing at the walls.

"Oh, those are actually collages. I make them in my spare time," Dr. Noham said, pointing to three side-by-side images of mystical women. "These three I call 'the sisters,' and I try to sell the others, but art doesn't sell well, so I end up giving them away to my friends. I have piles of them. Would you like one? Take your pick."

Embree aimed her trembling finger at one above the far desk, a beautiful woman garbed in a robe with a sunshine halo and blue-stylized background of shale between the cosmos.

"She hasn't changed much, doctor, except she's exhausted. She can't climb the stairs without collapsing."

"How is your sleep?" Dr. Noham asked.

"Most of the time, sixteen hours a day, except for one night of none earlier in the week, I think, right Embree?" Luke queried. "And another four hours of squirming around each day on the couch, miserable and trying to sleep."

"That's okay. Let her rest. Are you having suicidal thoughts, Embree?" Dr. Noham asked.

"Please kill me now," Embree said.

"Do you want to go to the hospital?"

"Absolutely not," Embree stuttered.

"So, this is unfortunate, but the lithium and valproic acid don't seem to be working if you're still having spurts of mixed mania, and extreme fatigue is a rare side effect from the aripiprazole, so we need to try something new. I have just the answer; this helps every person I've ever prescribed it to: lurasidone."

"It helped me, Bubs," Luke said.

Embree nodded, a sloth amongst the living.

"It's expensive—about sixty dollars a pill, before insurance—but I can't stress enough how good it is. Now, the half-life for aripiprazole is about seventy five hours, so you're going to be exhausted for a few more days once we switch over. Meet again in a month?"

Embree began taking a low dose of lurasidone that night to the sound of Clicky trilling somewhere in the cracks of the cottage, and all night he continued on and off.

Two weeks in, Embree began having panic attacks in

the evening after long days of extreme stress and restlessness, with the mixed mania heightening to a suicide-inducing peak. She paced and moaned, feeling almost as if her blood was boiling, especially in her chest and shins, and during the evenings Luke would drive her to get ice cream in downtown Maine past the school and all the little storefronts and gas stations, herself an effigy gasping for air in the nightly attacks and rolling the window up and down constantly in hopes that it would somehow help.

Embree began to count the seconds as the days passed, buried in the couch for hours after she woke, with the doctor doubling her dosage of lurasidone during the next visit. Sometimes her chest burned and felt stony like her heart pains from before, except this time around far worse—it felt as if there was a black hole where her heart should be, bowing her ribs in with its gravity to a point in pain where she had to sit, head collapsed into her arms, and where she would nearly pass out, huffing and woozy. One night, she rose from the couch after suffering a chest pain of stress and tension that redefined all her notions of pain, and she stumbled onward and fell to the floor, annihilated, before Luke could carry her back to the couch.

Two months in, the long periods of pain had numbed Embree, and she lashed out if she'd wake when Luke was asleep, crushing an apple with her palms, pacing, seeing a shadow-haired demon around most every corner, and attempting with all her strength to rip her hair out. She was always red-faced and crying from what seemed to her like the adrenaline and artery-bursting blood pressure alone pushing out the few sporadic tears. It was only now, overwhelmed in a way she could never conceive before, that she could no longer for the moment feel the pain of her past and, frankly, thought of it now as bullshit.

Luke had had enough and called Dr. Noham's emergency line one day, talking apart from Embree in his closed bedroom.

"Dr. Noham, Embree's almost dying. She can't even describe the pain she's in. She can't speak. She's restless but she's not really manic anymore."

"Well, you said something important. Now that her mania is capping off, I can introduce an antidepressant. Let's take lurasidone up to 120mg and introduce 20mg of fluoxetine to start."

"Right now?"

"Yes, I'll put the order in."

Embree suffered her nightly panic attacks like clockwork after long, horrifying days of seething, cataclysmal pain and confusion and suicidal yearning, taking her pills with Luke's help and guidance until the next session, where out of desperation and having never seen true mixed-state suffering, Dr. Noham prescribed the mood-stabilizing lurasidone at its maximum dosage: 160mg.

The following week, Embree fared no better and tried to kill herself one night by scraping a pen cap against her wrist in a fury, ultimately throwing it against the wall while lightheaded and fuming. Around dinnertime one night, her jaw became stuck open, and she tried to talk to Luke through her mouth agape, freaking out. Eventually, as he was about to call the doctor, the stiffness in her muscles subsided, and she continued on to her usual restless panic attack before she would pray to whoever to please for the love of whoever fall asleep, with one of the deer mounts staring down on her always. She became disinterested in everything—movies, television, and fishing included—and with all of her strength and in all the hopelessness adrift she resisted trying to kill herself again.

In the fourth month of lurasidone, through all the pain and the atomizing of every fiber of her being, beyond the evening cackling of early spring redwing blackbirds, the end of an era neared. Embree's jaw once again stiffened to the point where it wouldn't shut, and Luke, by her side, escorted her to the couch before which she slipped and fell onto his shoulder, him bearing her weight in its entirety. She collapsed onto the couch, twisting and twirling, her one leg stiffening upright at the hip, one of her arms becoming rigid, her jaw stuck and cramping painfully as she tried to blubber, and her chest tightening.

"I—," Embree muttered, writhing for relief, "I can't breathe."

Luke called an ambulance and then called Dr. Noham, disquieted by the pale knot before him and truly worried by the intensity of her choking that she may not make it through the night.

Dr. Noham sighed over the phone, saying one word, "dystonia," and then explaining that the lurasidone won't work and that she was so sorry and that Embree will need another drug and that "there's plenty of drugs left in the toolbox" and rescheduling her next appointment sooner and asking if they had diphenhydramine, which they only had a few ounces of in an ancient bottle in the kitchen cabinet, before ending the call. Embree slugged the few ounces of diphenhydramine, still twisting, and partial relief came before any emergency services appeared.

A state trooper arrived first and Luke had to explain

twice, showing evidence, that Embree was having a reaction to a prescribed medication—nothing illegal. Eventually, the trooper conceded and helped Luke carry the disoriented girl to the porch, where the medics were unfolding and locking open a stretcher. They heaved her onto the stretcher, lifted the stretcher into the ambulance as it scissored shut, turned on the lights and sirens, and Luke followed the ambulance to Wilson Hospital in his car.

"This arm—is that from the dystonia?" one medic asked.

"No, I'm just holding," Embree said, losing her breath, "it up—it up for fun, man. It's a fucking party in here."

The medics rushed to set up an intravenous injection of far more diphenhydramine than the bottle recommends as a dosage, pinching Embree with the needle and taping it in place and connecting all the tubing and finally inoculating her with the push of a plunger. The sirens sounded muffled to her, and the vehicle seemed to her as slow and bumpy as her recovery, if she'd ever recover at all, and soon her eyelids grew heavy, and she fell asleep.

Embree woke to the sound of the stretcher scissoring open, its wheels crashing against cold pavement, and the medics hurried her through sliding glass doors, past the nurse's station and all its curious glares, and into one of twelve cubicles partitioned off from one another by curtains—all assorted like slanted parking spaces—wheeling her to a smooth stop.

"The doctor will be with you in..." Embree heard before falling back asleep.

Embree woke several times to Luke staring and then finally to a white-coat woman looming over her, talking to Luke on and off about dystonia and asking if the psychiatrist had been informed and finally prescribing a week's worth of Trihexyphenidyl.

Embree then found herself walking and leaning into Luke's shoulder a little past midnight in the hospital parking lot under moonlit overcast and sleet. She swung low into the belly of his car, an era of poisoning gone by.

24

Embree fell out of belief with the axiom that time heals all wounds. Time had murdered her—spending almost four months laying, most of the time so restless and in pain that she had to count the seconds as they passed to distract herself from suicidal thoughts, had broken her spirit and shattered her mind. She was zombified, still laying into the couch most days and recounting the claustrophobia of the rapes and dystonia, breathing hard and shuddering.

The next drug to try was Risperidone, and Embree took it reluctantly the night the spring peepers appeared. Bullhead fishing would soon be at its finest, Luke knew, but he was too busy caring for her to smash the shit out of Whitney Point Reservoir for even one night. He recalled the night when he caught so many bullhead that, unhooking them, his fingers were skinned raw by their rough-toothed biting, and he remembered how in the morning the Amish boys came down the dirt road in their horse and carriage and stared, amazed, as he dragged from the shore an improvised rope stringer of exactly fifty bullhead.

Within a few days of taking Risperidone, Embree began violently shaking at the legs anytime she sat, bouncing at the knees and tapping the heels of her feet. Luke became concerned, calling the doctor, who worried about her developing "tardive dyskinesia," a rare and sometimes permanent condition of repetitive movement caused by long term use of neuroleptic drugs.

The following appointment was sobering. Embree was a depressed, calloused mess.

"Embree, how are you?" Dr. Noham asked.

Embree shook her head in disapproval.

"I have your bloodwork back," Dr. Noham said, sitting and struggling slightly to remember every unnoted detail due to juggling and servicing over three hundred patients. "Oh wait, I went over that last time. How is your sleep?"

"Too much—way too much."

"Are you restless? I see your legs stopped shaking as much."

"Always, at least a little. It never goes away," Embree said, red-faced and bordering on crying. "Please, for the love of God, help me or kill me." She predicted next the doctor would ask about death—sweet, seductive death.

"Are you having suicidal thoughts?"

"Yes."

"Do you have a plan?"

"Not really."

"Okay. Are you still having hallucinations?"

"Yes, yes, yes, yes, probably, okay, and sure—can I have my medicine now?"

Dr. Noham paused.

"We're not out, but we are running low on options. I like to use the newer stuff because it has less side effects."

Embree laughed derisively as she cried.

"I think you should try asenapine. Now, this drug is different. Instead of eating it, you take it sublingually—that is, letting it melt under your tongue after dinner, okay?"

"Umm, Okay?"

"Meet again in a few weeks?" Dr. Noham asked.

"Whatever."

That night Embree pried at the sample pack of asenapine from Dr. Noham's collection, digging out a chalky tablet from the blister pack. She put it under her tongue in view of Luke, squinting and wincing as it dissolved and burned. Afterward, everything felt to her the same.

Late that night, after a nap, Embree rose to take a piss, groping her way through the darkness past Vinny dripping and around the doorframe to the bathroom. She felt lightheaded, and suddenly she fell to the tiling as her knees buckled, and the last thing she heard and felt was gravity smashing her to the floor before facing a moment of darkness and then feeling Luke's calming hands on hers.

Dr. Noham gave Embree a brief break, worried about overwhelming her. Luke and Embree drove to their first visit of Dr. Mooney, LCSW-R and ACSW, crossing the great rusting trestle bridge of Vestal and past the newfound greenness of grass and wild onions beside the overpasses and budding locust trees and aspen here and there, beyond several multi-lane intersections. The building was a tall complex with a parking lot wrapped around it, and a sign detailed the therapists and others who worked inside, with a Jaguar parked conspicuously in the lot among other cars and sedans for this time and every time again that they'd return.

They entered the back door leading to carpeted steps down, turning left through a glass door to a room where oriental flute music played, a water and tea station stood, a secretary and her desk and computer lived in the corner, and wicker chairs and kaleidoscope rug ruled the back half. Embree recognized in an open cabinet the pictures of collages from Dr. Noham along with crystals, gemstone bracelets, and necklaces.

"Why hello," said the secretary.

"Hey," Luke said back.

A woman clothed in white shirt, jeans, and a beautiful light-blue shawl came clicking at the heels around the corner from a hallway, smiling and inviting Embree in with her hand. Luke stayed behind, and the therapist and Embree walked the carpeted hall together, entering a room with a desk neatly covered in paperwork and crystals, a leather sofa with a box of tissues by the window, and across from that an ergonomic recliner and ottoman and oak stand.

"Please, sit. You're Embree, right?"

"Yes."

"How are you doing?"

"Worse than you could possibly imagine."

"Well, the first thing I should say is I may not be the right fit for you, and that's okay. You have to decide that. So, what's troubling you?"

"I have severe mixed mania, depression, and psychosis; I've been raped twice, not counting being molested before all that; I watched my boyfriend die; and every medicine I try is killing me. The only people I have on my side are Luke and Dr. Noham; otherwise, I'd be dead right now."

"Wow, okay—that's awful, I'm so sorry. You're distressed still by the rapes and death, right? Have you ever heard of dialectical behavioral therapy?"

"Yes, no."

"Well, honestly, I think it would be helpful for everyone on the planet, but it really shines with cases of PTSD. Are you comfortable telling me about these incidents?"

"Rod Bennet and his asshole friends raped me. My

boyfriend died against a guard rail with his brains hanging out. Then, when I was homeless a DEC officer raped me."

"An officer?!"

"Yes," Embree cried.

"Wow, unbelievable—I mean, I believe you, but wow. Embree, I have tissues right there if you need them."

Embree took a tissue, wiped her eyes, and blew her nose.

"Okay, so, Embree, what's happening in PTSD is your flight or fight response becomes overactive. It's normally helping you keep safe, but in these cases it's crossing the line. What triggers these attacks? It's important to become aware of triggers."

"I love Luke," Embree diverted, "and I want to be able to touch him and him to touch me. He deserves better than me. But it's so hard."

"Don't worry, we'll work on it until you're healed. We have to explore what meaning you attach to these things, like touching, in order for you to gain back control."

The session went on for an hour, with Embree mostly sobbing over the rapes and pain of the mixed mania and Jason's death over and over and Dr. Mooney letting her vent.

Cariprazine was next. Within three weeks, it gave Embree nighttime akinesia where she'd roll, squirm at the legs, and wring her hands for hours while laying along the couch, unable to stop for more than a few seconds at a time.

Afterword, quetiapine was up to bat, and Dr. Noham hated quetiapine and made obvious to them her disdain for it, but out of desperation she gave it a shot. Quetiapine was a prisoner's medicine, Embree found out—the number one commodity in prisons for its quality of making people sleep away the time. Embree slept through spring, twenty hours a day, breaking free of the pain of mixed mania and trading it for the lesser pain of deep depression, where she'd wake up every morning from the couch weeping, pacing, eating, and weeping some more in several bursts throughout her short day, sometimes for up to an hour. She lived on the couch, beginning to become less bitchy but also gaining twenty pounds at the hips and breasts and belly from her cravings until she ballooned into something she hated, still not telling Luke of the rapes, together in effect but separated deep down.

PART 5

25

Dr. Noham worked on the delicate balance between antidepressant and mood stabilizer, gradually increasing Embree's fluoxetine to 40mg and then 60mg, lifting her from severe to moderate depression where she'd sob once a day when she woke and feel bummed out in general instead of weeping four times a day and feeling tantalizingly suicidal throughout. The doctor finally gave up on quetiapine, using it as a placeholder of sorts all this time, in exchange for a sample pack of an experimental drug, brexpiprazole, which wasn't originally designed to treat bipolar disorder, but the doctor had found through the ever-growing grape vine that some researchers recommended it as an antipsychotic and mood stabilizer. She started with 1mg tablets of brexpiprazole, increasing after two weeks, adding alprazolam for her anxiety, and removing benztropine due to reading issues and double vision.

In three weeks, the brexpiprazole and alprazolam began to take effect, calming her and dampening her depression and lessening her stupefying rate of hallucinations, and Luke invited his friends, Jake and Erin, over for a bonfire to meet Embree and support her throbbing upward climb and celebrate her partial revival.

Late spring had passed with its mayapples like little designer umbrellas, its morel mushrooms, its spring peepers and gray treefrogs calling and trilling, and its puddle-spotted pastures, making way for early summer with its grasshoppers, drying vegas, and croaking toads.

Luke carried old firewood from a stack behind the

house, hauling it down to the shore of Nanticoke creek and heaping it in the young hay and thistle. As night fell and the sun collapsed for starlight, two pickup trucks peeled down Ames Road, one flicking a cigarette that burst in embers onto the road, all of which Embree saw from her foldup chair. Three more chairs were positioned around the logs and a growing collection of tinder. She heard the truck doors slam, and Luke lit the tinder afire with its small flames licking and climbing and gluing themselves to the midsized sticks as it all spat a dull roar.

"Hey!" Erin exclaimed.

Jake waved, emerging in the distant glow of the young fire.

"Hey, how are you guys?" Luke asked, looking up.

"We're great!"

"Have a seat guys," Luke said, setting the split logs into the flames. "I'll go get the hotdogs and marshmallows."

"So, you're Embree, right? Luke told us all about you."

Ever-bold, Embree was calm and pensive tonight.

"Well, not everything, I hope," Embree chuckled.

"We're Erin, Jake," Erin said.

"You're a fisherwoman?" Jake asked.

"Yes, an ex-charter fisherwoman and I guess some kind of partner now with his videos."

"Oh, I bet Luke loves you then," Erin cheered.

Luke returned with a pack of hotdogs, buns, a bag of marshmallows, shot glasses, and a bottle of tequila.

"Are you guys playing nice?"

"Yes, babydoll," Embree said warmly, pausing. "How long have you two been together?"

"Oh, we're not together. I mean, we used to be, but now we're just friends," Jake clarified. "Last time we were together was way back when Luke was falling apart from his OCD."

"The OCD, right, yeah," Embree said. "Luke, what did you mean months ago when you said you'd scare me away with the OCD?"

"Oh, shit—I'm sorry Luke," Jake said. "I figured we all knew."

Luke sighed, pausing. "Time to ruin the mood. I didn't expect this to come up tonight."

"Please—I'll tell you what's wrong with me; what's bothering me."

"In all honesty," Luke said, "I don't remember telling anyone besides my doctor about the OCD."

"You told us a long time ago," Jake said.

"When? I don't remember that."

"When we were fishing with that Jason kid in Forks."

"Jason?" Embree asked. "Jason who?!"

"Newton, maybe?" Jake said.

"Newfield?" Embree asked.

"Maybe," Jake added.

"I thought his name was Mason," Luke said.

"Oh my God, you've got to be kidding me. He's my old boyfriend, the one who took me up here in the first place," Embree said, choking up. "He died. I was with him."

"Man, Embree, I'm so sorry," Luke said, pausing. "I'd forgotten the name. He was a great bass and walleye fisherman. I only met him once, but he showed me that spot in Forks."

"The beautiful place?"

"I don't know what's so beautiful about it. Maybe you're thinking of a different spot."

"Damnit," Embree said. "It was in the fall, Jason said—

the beautiful part. I always wanted to see that place."

"I'll take you there sometime," Luke said. "I was an asshole back in high school. They knew me as the Bringle, and I was a lucky bastard, but those are stories for another time. Do you still want to know about the OCD?"

"Yes," Embree said. "Thank you. I just, like, sidetracked hard—wow."

"Okay so traditional OCD, obsessive-compulsive disorder, involves thoughts that cause anxiety and rituals that the person does to try to alleviate that anxiety, right?

"It's all new to me, Luke," Embree said. "But, I mean, that probably sucks, I know, especially if you're hurt by it, but it doesn't sound like something that would scare someone off. Do you know what I mean?"

"Yes, Bubs, but let me finish. I had that type of OCD when I was younger, and it did suck. I washed my hands raw and repeated these stupid shit lines and counted to try to save myself from my worries. But that's not the part people don't understand."

"What is?" Embree inquired.

"It's called pure-o, short for pure-obsessional OCD. I had that too, later."

"What does that mean?" Embree asked.

Erin and Jake leaned in, one roasting marshmallows on a stick and the other a burning a hotdog on a handheld spit, listening intently.

"Pure-o is a manifestation of OCD where the sufferer fears he's going to hurt or kill people, and it traumatizes him."

"You want to kill people?" Embree asked.

"No, see, that's what everyone thinks," Luke said calmly, "but that's really the opposite of what I want. The last thing I want to do is hurt someone, but my mind would bully me with pure-o by giving me graphic intrusive thoughts of me hurting or killing who I care about most."

"Do you have them about me?" Embree asked.

"Do I care about you?" Luke asked, tongue-in-cheek.

"I see," Embree said. "Well, Luke, drumroll please: I still love you. And I still can't believe you guys knew Jason."

"I'm sorry, Embree; I just didn't recognize the..."

"I've been raped," Embree interrupted.

"Huh, who...what?!" Luke asked.

"It's okay if you don't want to touch me anymore," Embree added. "I'm sorry I hid it for so long."

"No, Embree, I love you. You did nothing wrong. All I want is to lay hands on this whoever..."

"Rod Bennet," Embree interrupted again. "And a DEC officer."

"Twice?!"

"Yes, on the low end—sorry."

"Embree, stop apologizing goddamnit," Luke said, growing impatient for the first time in years. "You didn't do anything wrong!"

"Thanks, Bubs. I'm sorry I upset you."

"Embree!" Luke exclaimed.

"Oh, right," Embree muttered.

Everyone paused. An ember flew into the bag of marshmallows and made an awful squeal in the dead night with nothing to soothe it but a lone cicada and the running of the stream.

"Wow, both of you," Erin said. "Both of you, I'm so sorry. You guys need a vacation or something."

They all paused for another minute.

"Look at you two love birds. I need a fucking

girlfriend," Jake said.

"Is that an operative use of the word 'fucking?'" Erin asked facetiously.

26

Days later, the sun rose against a daisy chain of gold-crowned altocumulus clouds, reddening at their hearts. Taking Erin's suggestion, Luke and Embree decided to go on vacation with most of their meager savings funds. They packed camera and fishing gear, swimwear and other clothes, and survival gear in black-blue duffel bags, loading them into the car. They lit up the roadways, taking East Maine Road to Airport Road to NY-17 East through the rolling wilderness of the Catskills and down past Newburgh, switching to I-87 South and then I-95 North along the tidal estuary of Long Island Sound, arriving in Norwalk, Connecticut.

The pier was short and sand-crusted and they walked the creaky planks out to the boat with Luke's rich aunt and uncle and their two daughters, the family club members of a private island. Loading their gear, they then crammed into the boat and rode the wavelets of the strait six-hundred yards to the island, during high tide, where they docked and unloaded before the boat returned, shrinking in their view as it went.

"Thank you guys for having us," Luke said to his aunt, uncle, and three year old twin cousins.

"Anytime, ya bastard," the uncle said back.

"William!" exclaimed the aunt.

"We gotta have fun but also pump out some videos, Bubs. This place is a survivalist's gold mine. That is what you do best—that's your thing—right?"

Embree nodded, stretching her arms out to the beautiful vista.

As the tide lowered and after Luke set down his bags at a campsite near the middle and gave her the tour, Embree found the island was shaped almost like a swimming turtle. The long sandbar of a tail jutted to one side of the rear of a forested, near-circle carapace, with little lawns and jetties off the beaches forming the legs and a wooded bluff on the opposite end taking shape as the head. The island was infested with poison ivy deep in the scrub and along some of the foot trails—a nuisance that was managed by the club personnel, albeit not perfectly. Spiders, mice, and insects had invaded the leaf litter, limbs, and craggy rockwork between beaches. The salty air warmed their faces, and the skyline was a cornucopia of gold-fringed forest, shimmering waves, a full sun, and glinting shale past the sandbar.

Luke had already strapped a camera to his chest, having changed into his trunks and encouraging Embree to change into her bikini.

"Oh, you look stunning, babe. These vids are gonna be banging."

Embree's taut waist with two indents on either side of her abs met the curves of her hips and the skirt over her ass flawlessly—a look she'd fasted for all month—and her pronounced collarbone crowned her breasts cupped in red cloth. The restraints of Luke's camera wound around his muscled shoulders and his abs, spiderwebbing out in four straps above blue trunks that drifted with the breeze about his knees. He walked with his camera on, her ahead of him, exploring.

Sea glass smoothened with time laid among the countless grains of sand, all along a swimming beach where people congregated and which was skirted on either side by shale escarpments, which Embree and Luke approached, with their footsteps washing away with the sloshing waves.

"Look, Bubs, mussels!" Luke shouted, "But they're ridged mussels—no good to eat."

Grayish mussels with crests and valleys along their sides clung to the moist shale in a little colony.

"What about these, Bubs?" Embree said, pointing toward the shoreline.

A cluster of iridescent blue mussels gripped the rocks.

"Blue mussels, jackpot! These, folks, are delicious. We'll cook these up with whatever else we find."

Embree and Luke pried with their fingertips the mussels from the rocks, collecting them on film into a small backpack that Luke was carrying and slung over his shoulder. Empty oyster shells washed and teetered ashore. They scaled the bluff like spider monkeys, rock climbing by clenching hands and fitting their toes in cracks, reaching the other side with its green kelp spilling to-and-fro from the underwater drop-off onto a flat of shale. Rocks littered the tidal pools, and she began to bend over and flip them, carrying on for most of fifteen minutes.

"Hey, come look at this!" Embree said.

In a pool, beside a flipped rock in the brackish water, sidestepped an orangish figure bigger than both of her fists put together, and she plunged her paw in and grabbed it, unknowing at the moment what it was or if it was venomous. She lifted the lobster from the pool with a triumphant squeal and held it over her head as it thrashed its tail and slipped through her hands, its body a tiddlywink falling and tumbling back into the ocean and the claws, having broken off, still firmly gripped in her hand.

"Ah, well damn, Emb, we almost had lobster tail!"

"Motherfucker," Embree said, fitting the claws in the backpack.

Embree flipped rocks for another fifteen minutes but only found barnacles. She raked the kelp with her hands on film and found the inch-long, springing glass shrimp flicking themselves ashore in the slosh of the waves, and she swatted three of them up onto the drier shale and picked one up, crunching and eating it raw with her lips pursed and eyes closed, facing the camera.

"You're wild, Bubs," Luke said. "These vids are gonna be short but killer. I can feel it."

They put away the camera and swam in the swimming zone off the beach for a while, the sun scathing and casting high shadows, with others, including the twins in their floaties, splashing and frolicking nearby.

In the evening, Embree snuck onto the bluff with the backpack and some tinder and lit a gentle fire in a crevasse, careful to keep the smoke light and wispy. In the embers, she cooked the lobster claws and then the blue mussels, sizzling, Luke by her side, the horizon embroidered with purples and reds and a crescent sun.

They slept together in a tent by Luke's family after Embree took her pills, the starlight dim against the fabric and William snoring off to the side.

"Luke," Embree whispered. "Luke, Luke!"

"What's up, Emb?" Luke said groggily, twisting.

"I have a riddle for you."

"Huh? The fuck?"

"What's a little heaven when you're going to hell anyway?"

"Again—huh?" Luke chuckled.

"Come with me," Embree urged, holding out a hand.

They walked wooded trails, breaking the nighttime spider webs, and then they strolled the beach, making out at Embree's insistence, tied together at the hips, and finally they quietly dragged their feet into the restricted zone of midnight beach and lowered themselves into the thrashing waves and made love for the first time in the moonlit seascape, swaying in the surf, their trunks and bikini washing ashore amongst the twinkling sea glass. Embree for once enjoyed it, gasping amid the salty spray.

The following day, Embree woke sore but delighted with sand in the cracks of her bikini. Luke woke, too, at her insistence and the rubbing of his shoulder.

"Mornin' beautiful, what's up?" Luke asked.

"I don't know. You wanna go film?"

"Yeah, we should make the best of it while we're here. What time is it?"

"Around sunrise."

"Let's go fish for stripers on the sandbar. They push the bunker up into the bar around now. It's a lot of fun."

"Okay, blubbers," Embree said, smiling and rocking his limp shoulders.

They moved down past the one-man bodega near the entrance pier, cutting carefully past arms of poison ivy to the turtle's tail and watching the striped bass swirl, rise, and churn, rushing and pinching the schools of bunker up against the shoreline of the sandbank jetty. Embree tossed out a popper on a walleye rod, watching a bass jump on and inhale it almost immediately, and she leaned into the fish as it made its runs, finally wresting it ashore on film.

"Here's a nice little striper, folks," Embree cheered,

squatting as she held the fish, smiling, and squinting in the rising sunlight.

They caught several more stripers as a team before the bunker disappeared and the bass moved away, including one large thirty-inch keeper that Embree wrestled with its tail slapping against her breasts, and she ripped its gills out before dropping it on the sandbar, bleeding and soon lifeless.

"What's that, Bubs?" Embree asked, rushing down the sandbar as the tide slowly but surely rose, watching water spit like a fountain into the air.

Embree began to dig with her claws, Luke filming, the sand spitting up in her face, and after scooping out a trench of wet sand, she felt the hard shell of a clam as it withdrew itself into its shell and closed tight.

"Clams!" Embree shouted.

The ocean was rising, leaving just a thin strip of sand to return on, but before they returned, they found three more clams, digging together, hurrying, and they added them to their backpack, walking back through the shallows and spotting a horseshoe crab and a leopard crab waddling away in the surf.

They grilled the clams and striper fillets and the awkward horseshoe crab against the fierce sun and sloshing of the rising tide.

"This has been the best trip ever—thanks, my Bubs," Embree said.

"Oh, this is just the beginning. I love you, Emb."

27

Early summer blew by like the accompanying breeze. Embree visited Dr. Noham and Dr. Mooney several times over, finally gaining ground before losing it again.

"Embree," Dr. Noham said, "this time in your life, this recovery you've had, will continue. Think of it as two steps forward and one step back. It's a process, and you will get better, just as you were."

"Dr. Noham, I feel like fucking killing myself again."

"Do you have a plan?"

"No, but I wish I fucking did," Embree said, sighing. "Everything hurts so damn bad after so much pain. It's like I'm hypersensitive to it. I can't take one more drop."

"I think we can safely raise your fluoxetine to 80mg per day at this point, a max dose, but it will take a few weeks to kick in, okay?"

"Okay," Embree said.

"What about supplements?" Luke asked from the side. "Is she taking fish oil?"

"No," Embree said.

"Oh, dear, I apologize—I should've mentioned that long ago. Fish oil improves brain health. Please, take two capsules in the evening, 2200mg total."

"Anything else?" Luke asked.

"I'd recommend Ashwagandha—also two capsules in the evening, 2000mg total. It reduces stress, improves memory, and may lower depression, too."

"Thank you, Dr. Noham," Luke said. "Thank you for always being good to us."

"Oh, well you guys are both very welcome. Embree,

call my personal line if you have any serious problems. Everything should get better with time, okay?"

"Okay," Embree said.

Over the next few weeks, Embree moaned on the couch out of scathing boredom and shuffled about the cottage, tired, and she became teary-eyed, but she didn't weep once.

In three weeks, Embree began to feel the difference, hugging Luke so tightly in the rank of his computer-bound must that he choked and had to peel her off of him.

"You smell like shit. Take a shower, man."

"Later—I'm editing our beach trip, Bubs."

Luke had divided the trip into seven videos: finding mussels, catching a lobster, fire making and cooking, digging clams, catching stripers, outtakes, and horseshoe crab catch-and-cook. He gave each a clickbait title, wherein nobody could resist clicking and investigating, and on each he added thorough tags and a description and used custom thumbnails of Embree holding the catch and squatting in her bikini.

"These are gonna be winners, Bubs," Luke said, clicking around maniacally with messy hair and his favorite stained t-shirt.

Embree paused, staring. The whole time they'd been talking, Luke hadn't broke eye contact with the computer.

"Is that what this is all about?" Embree asked.

"Is what all about?"

"This, the videos."

"You're making no sense, babe," Luke said, still clicking intensely.

"You used me."

"What?" Luke paused. "Now I'm really losing you."

"These, Luke, look at me goddamnit!" Embree shouted, holding her breasts. "You used me for these. You knew they'd get views."

"No...no, no—Embree, I swear."

"It's all about your precious fucking gold play button, isn't it?"

"Dude," Luke said, "come on, please, seriously?"

"Fuck you; you knew I'd be pretty camera fodder. That stupid button means more to you than me, doesn't it?"

Embree stormed off and laid on the couch, feet hanging from the edge, her head buried in the crack between cushions, defeated and with absolutely nowhere to turn. She thought about drowning herself in the creek somehow, and then Luke followed her into the room.

"What's your problem, babe?"

"I don't fucking care anymore; that's my fucking problem," Embree said, muffled by the cushion. "Or maybe that's my solution."

"Hey, no suicide jokes, okay?"

"You wish it was a joke. Go away," Embree cried. "I don't want to hear it."

"Emb, a lot of people depend on me. I interact with them. I've turned a lot of people's lives around."

"So?"

"This work has helped a lot of people out of bad places. There was a time when I was a small channel and before things got so crazy that I'd fish with kids with disabilities—and host events—such as physical disabilities, Asperger's, depression, and down's syndrome, to name a few, and I'd make their day if not more than that. Those people still depend on me."

"But what about me?"

"I love you, Emb."

"Then prove it."

"How?"

"Spend some time with just me. I need someone. I need someone now. I need you.

"I'm here, Bubs. Would you like me to take the videos down?"

"No, all I wanted was to just hear those words—that I'm more important than your life's work. You're all I've got and all I will ever have, my last chance."

"I swear to God, Bubs, I'll quit YouTube today if it means not losing you."

"Okay."

"Here, come rest with me, my Bubs," Luke said, waving Embree on. "I won't touch you."

They both got into separate sides of Luke's king-sized bed, pulling over the covers, and Embree stopped sniffling.

"Wow, Luke, your bed is so damn comfy. I love it. And you can touch me anytime. I don't mind. I'm past that."

"I just wanted to be sure, and I know it's comfy, Emb. Why do you think I wanted you to have it in the first place? I wanted the best for you."

"There wasn't much love in my house," Embree said, veering.

"What do you mean, Bubs?"

"My mom, when she was still alive, she was great—she treated me with independence and love and tried to protect me when I needed it."

"I'm sorry she's gone," Luke said.

"But my father, he was fucking terrible. He'd always get drunk and yell and demand shit and give nothing back. One time he got drunk and mad at me and pulled me by my hair down the stairs, and I was screaming. It was terrible," Embree said, pausing. "Before I just wanted to be free, and now that I am free, I just want for once in my godforsaken life to be loved."

"Bubs," Luke said, choking up. "I love you, Bubs. You're my best friend, and I would do anything for you, promise. We'll take a long break from filming—maybe retire, okay?"

"Thanks—I love you, too."

28

In the midnight stir a heavy rain fell, and through the window and by the crack and flash of a bolt of lightning Embree saw a big buck—too big to count its tines, standing by Luke's run-down shed—and then it was gone with the darkness and pitter-patter of rain. She stood in awe for a moment, returning to washing the dishes.

"You know, Bubs," Embree said, "I know where you're coming from. Maybe we should go back to your roots."

"What do you mean?"

"You know, like holding events for the disabled. Helping people, just helping people, and not worrying about the next great thing. We just gotta figure out how to pay for it."

"Yeah, Emb, I totally dig it. We could travel. And maybe we don't have to figure out the money."

"What do you mean?"

"Remember those beach vids we made?" Luke asked.

"Yeah..."

"They exploded, Emb, especially the horseshoe crab catch-and-cook. I've read the comments. They love you and your wild side. You're famous."

"Wow, well congrats!"

"They're your videos, Emb. I just edited them. You're the star, and the money is yours to do with as you wish."

"How much money?"

"A lot—tens of thousands extra and counting."

"Holy shit."

"Yeah, and it's yours to do whatever you want with."

"Travel?"

"If you want, absolutely."

That night Embree showered and pinned up her hair and wore a beautiful, teal, dreamlike dress and had Luke set up a livestream with his webcam, which thousands of people instantly joined and cheered through text in the chat box, idolizing her magnificence, attitude, wildness, and the brunette waves falling past her shoulders.

"Howdy y'all, I'm Embree and this is Luke from L.B. Outdoors. We have an exciting announcement, so we thought we'd livestream tonight. We're going to be visiting one city a year to fish with anyone who wants to come, and anyone with a physical or mental disability will be eligible for special prizes like signed t-shirts and free guided fishing trips from yours truly. My question is—and you can answer in the chat box—which city should we visit first."

The chat box went ballistic, the text rocketing.

"I think I see Philadelphia the most. I'll prepare the permit, and I can't wait to see you guys there! I love you all! Luke will make a post-video about when and where exactly. It'll be at least one whole day, maybe next weekend! Bring anything you want us to sign, and bring your fishing gear!"

A week later, Embree and Luke were dolled up and exiting the airport with their duffel bags and sunglasses in the early morning shafts of light peeking from the skyline, finding and packing and entering their rental car: a humble blue Rav4.

They drove through the Philadelphia morning commute and gridlock to the banks of the Schuylkill River, a mowed park zone with niceties like railings over the bank, trash cans, and gingko saplings scattered about. A crowd of over a hundred people had gathered, talking among themselves, then cheering and clapping and whistling as Luke and Embree opened their doors in the nearby parking lot, her makeup perfect and the light glinting white off her sunglasses. They brought with them their duffel bags, strutting toward the crowd and beaming.

"Hello, Philadelphia!" Embree shouted.

Still, people were coming from the lot in the morning light and would continue to all day, and runners and dog walkers passing by along the bridge looked down at the spectacle, staring.

"How y'all doing?"

The crowd cheered.

"I'm Embree and this is my boyfriend, Luke, host of L.B. Outdoors!"

The bridge was supported by stonework pillars, and the gingkos blushed and twirled at the leaves in the gentle gusts of the marvelous day, Embree noticed. Consumed by pain, she let the little things before disappear from her view; but now she soaked it all in, relishing moments so tiny and fading like dandelion seeds in the breeze. A few parking garages, town halls, and skyscrapers, most clean and shining, stood past the distant shore opposite the river.

Cheery, Embree announced to the crowd what was on her mind.

"Everyone, I haven't shared this, but Luke here saved my life. He's the greatest guy I ever met. He gave me a home, took me to the doctor, picked up my pieces...he saved me. Let's hear it for Luke!"

Almost everyone clapped and smirked, and Luke blushed.

"Bubs, thank you—you're so sweet, but, seriously, you

don't have to."

Embree walked around to the guests, shaking their hands and hugging many, as Luke followed her and did the same, chatting in little cliques—the Philadelphian families and outlying visitors that sacrificed during their long drives in.

Embree kneeled before a wheelchair-bound kid with cerebral palsy, his hand clenched and warped upright and his head twisted askew, grinning a toothy smile and his parents behind him, smiling.

"This is Jonathan, Embree and Luke—he's your biggest fan," the father said.

Embree's heart melted and mended and she grew teary-eyed holding the kid's little hand, and she reached into the duffel bag and pulled out a custom t-shirt in size small with "L.B. Outdoors" on the back and a vicious fish skeleton swirling on a popper on the front.

"Now you'll be the coolest kid in school, Jonathan," Embree said, "if you aren't already."

"T-ank you," Jonathan muttered, squealing in his excitement.

Embree remembered her dystonia while gazing at Jonathan and she shuddered but then recalled her therapist's advice to "take space" and separate herself from the panic and dread, breathing.

"I went through some very hard times, Jonathan. I bet we both have. But you don't have to let it define you, be your identity," Embree said, starting to choke up. "You can be anything you dream, buddy."

Embree kissed Jonathan on the cheek and moved on.

29

Four weeks after the Philadelphia trip, Luke was trying to hide a deadly grin, puckering his lips.

"I know that look. What is it?" Embree asked, digging.

"Remember those beach videos?"

"Yeah...we talked about them, Bubs. They're doing well, I know."

"Well about a week ago they went mega viral, even more viral than before, and with that comes the money, and with the money comes the power to help Jonathans everywhere. I've been waiting to show you. I knew this would be coming in the mail."

Luke held up a package addressed from Google headquarters, knowing it could only be one thing. Digging with a knife, he mined out a rectangular frame with the shining gold play button sitting decorous against whiteness behind a Plexiglas pane.

"Congrats, Luke! I love you, honey."

"You know what I love?" Luke asked.

"Me?"

"Yes, you," Luke said, dramatically stepping on the pedal of the trashcan and tossing the play button away.

They had sex on the wooden floor to the sounds of morning bobolinks and katydids chirping and trilling through the window.

Days later, a seriousness crossed Embree and she sat on the couch, just thinking—no television, no distractions.

"Luke, can we go to NYC?"

"Of course, Bubs. We can literally go anywhere. How's tomorrow sound?"

"Today," Embree said.

"Okay, I'll drive," Luke affirmed.

It was still morning and the redwing blackbirds cackled from their treetop roosts, and a murder of crows cawed and squabbled in the distance. The drive to the city was long and tedious, with morons jamming themselves in-between Luke's car and the car ahead and behind him amidst the gridlock of the expressway transitions. The tolls were fun, Embree thought in so many words. Many things were fun now.

In Brooklyn, Embree and Luke parallel parked and walked several streets down to Jason's old apartment — her hesitating, then knocking on door with three raps. Hailey answered.

"Hey, do I know you?"

"We've met, Hailey," Embree said.

"Oh, okay, what's up?"

"Do you know where Tim lives?"

"Tim the smoker, Tim the hustler, or Tim the writer?"

"Tim the writer."

"Just three blocks down—the apartment with the red-brick basement across from the graffiti."

"Thank you," Embree said.

Embree and Luke walked until they found what seemed like Tim's flat, the bricks a much richer and blacker red than they imagined and the graffiti much smaller, too. The streets were a dream state of honks, hollering, clacking steps along sidewalks and through intersections, and the faint smells of bakeries and food stalls wafting from down the way a half mile or more.

Embree rapped on Tim's door.

"This is what I came all this way for, Bubs. He's gotta

be home."

Nobody answered.

"I swear to God, I'll wait here on this porch all day," Embree said.

Finally the door opened a crack two minutes in and an eyeball peered through. Embree heard a chain swing loose, and the door swung wide open.

"Embree, is that you? What the fuck, man? I thought you were dead. I mean, I put money on it, and I won. Who's this? What happened to Jason?"

"I'm alive. Jason's up there somewhere," Embree said, pointing up. "This is Luke."

"How do ya do," Luke said, holding out his hand.

Tim shook Luke's hand at Luke's insistence, albeit halfheartedly, still gazing into Embree's face.

"Are you really Embree?" Tim asked, confused.

"The one and only. Tim, you're the only one who knows what happened that night."

"Oh," Tim said, turning. "Come with me. I guess if any-one deserves to know, it's you."

Tim walked past a catacomb of papers and notes and dirty dishes and a table with plot maps strewn about in the combined kitchen and living area. A replica of The Starry Night hung from a wall. Embree spotted a half-full glass of red wine—some things never change.

Tim reached into a drawer of a nightstand in his bed-room, shuffling, piling stacks of paper and sticky note packs and used sticky notes aside, until he found the party's bible — his drunken masterpiece of a notepad. Flip-ping through it, he found pictures of tigers, confused scrib-blings, signatures from those who thought he a famous writer, vodka and ice cream cake stains, and an overview of the gritty details in size thirty-two font, with twelve words per page over seventy-something pages. He paged through all of it.

"Yeah," Tim paused. "I just wanted to be sure. Jason knocked Rod out cold and we walked him down the stairs and sidewalk, perched between us on our shoulders. A homeless man sitting to the side asked if he was okay, and we told him he was just drunk and we were getting him home. Jason left him in an empty alleyway, his mouth open under a gutter with it beginning to sprinkle, and I remember his final words to me: 'We'll let God decide what to do with him.'"

"Wow, so he lied to me. He killed Rod."

"Kind of, yes, and kind of, no. The nature of this fucking industrial complex took its course."

"Where's Owen and Vitoria?"

"Why?"

"Because I want to talk to them?"

"About what?"

Embree paused.

"I want to forgive them."

"Well, Owen moved away to god-knows-where, and Vitoria bought the fast track to Hell."

"What do you mean?"

"Vitoria killed herself."

"Oh my God," Embree said.

Embree visited Allison's tombstone on her way out, choking up and showing Luke and asking the new caretaker where Boone was. The caretaker pointed to a neglected headstone in the far corner. The headstone read "Crocker Boone Cooke, He Was Not a Nice Man But He Did Good Deeds," and she shook her head in disbelief.

30

The midday sun scorched the Earth, a late September swell, with the sun surrounded by what seemed to Embree like a halo shining and stratus clouds over the far mountains. She was finally feeling stable and free, and upon her last visit, Dr. Noham had spaced out appointments to six-month intervals—a major milestone, one which Luke thought to celebrate the only way he knew.

"How about we go to Forks today, Bubs?" Luke asked.

"The beautiful place?!"

"Yes...you still love him, don't you?"

"Luke, no—come on."

"It's okay, Emb. You can tell me the truth."

"I miss him—I guess in a way I do love him, his memory, but more importantly I'm in love with you.

Luke blushed.

"Okay, but don't keep your hopes up, Emb. I seriously don't know what's so beautiful about this place, if it's even the right place."

"It's gotta be. How many spots are there in Forks?"

"At least a few, but there's only one I've fished with Jason—a secret hole, guarded, in the middle of fucking nowhere."

"Sounds like his sort of place to me," Embree said.

They hopped into the car with sprayed mud contrasting its glossy finish, fishing backpack and poles loaded and camera gear left behind, tearing down Ames Road and hitting switchback roads—Dunham Hill Road to Castle Creek, Route 11, and Knapp Hill Road—to the small town of Chenango Forks with its two bridges, one fire station, one gas station, one bar, and stoplight.

They burned down a seasonal dirt road, potholed and tight from archway limbs of oaks and silver maples, and they splashed through puddles at forty for over a mile, skirting the Chenango River beyond the great pool behind Davy's Bar, beyond the frothy confluence of the Chenango and Tioughnioga Rivers, and beyond the swampy canals on the left side of the road through which merchants used to row.

At the road's end was a dilapidated house on a wooded knoll, the driveway to which was cordoned off by caution tape, with several posted signs scattered about and a green figure like a monolith at the road's end guarding behind it a trail.

"See, this is the funny part, Bubs," Luke said, grabbing all the gear. "The trail is owned by the state park, but immediately to either side is owned by this asshole, so there's posted signs most of the way down. We'll be alright. People bike and walk their dogs on this every weekend."

They walked the trail down a quarter mile—past briars, scrub, and chirping chipmunks; past leaf litter to either side and down a hard-worked pebble path; and past a dead log with late-blooming dryad's saddle—and they arrived, sweating in the early fall heatwave, at an opening where the trail split in two, one way going into fir forest along the river and the other way traveling up a clearing of grass along more pines.

They veered into the firs, Embree following Luke, fishing gear in hand, dodging the trail's edge of three-leaved ivy, and they worked their way down a bluff to the rocky shore of the Chenango River, through thistle, sawgrass, goldenrod, and around small pockets of saplings and brush.

They walked down past the riffles to where the slack split free along a harsh current break, stepping over a rotting snapping turtle carcass, the few leaves of early-fading aspen caught in the flow, and they waded out side by side until the water, still slack, reached their belly buttons, tying onto their lines tube jigs from Luke's pocket.

"Now, just try drifting them, Emb. Let the current take them."

Embree casted out first at Luke's insistence and gesturing, letting the jig flow on its own accord through the riffling and shimmering main current, and on the second cast she felt a tap and leaned into it, watching a piglet of a smallmouth bass jump and twist in the distance, taking drag and drawing away from her in spurts.

"Oh, you've got a fighter on, baby!" Luke said, jesting.

"Oh," Embree laughed. "I know how to fish, buddy."

Embree fought the fish skillfully, letting it work itself tired, and brought the three-pound bass to her hand where it writhed, and she eventually palmed it, prying free the hook and plunking it back into the river.

"Maybe this is what Jason meant—their tiger stripes, maybe that's what's so beautiful."

"I don't know, Bubs—then why this spot?" Luke asked. "I can name ten other spots locally where we could catch these, and I'm sure Jason knew that, too."

They caught fifteen bass as the sun ebbed—Embree's nine to Luke's six—falling below the treetops in its gilded-skyline splendor.

"That's kind of beautiful," Embree said, pointing to the sunset's afterglow.

"Eh, I guess, Emb, but can't you see that anywhere, too?"

"I guess...," Embree sighed.

In the fading light, after the spot had seemed to be fished out, Embree hooked into a monstrous bass, eyeing its wakes as it veered, burned drag, and sped off into the distance, slapping the water in an explosion for every time it jumped, and boy, did it jump. It jumped ten times or more, threatening to spool her, before she began to turn it, tautening the six-pound line to its breaking point.

In time, like with her illnesses, Embree smoothed over the bass and it flopped toward her, seeing in the darkness it halfheartedly jumping one last time and lying on its side and hoisted to the top of the water, five pounds at least and over twenty-one inches, by her estimate and Luke's.

"Oh my God, Emb," Luke said, pointing his phone's flashlight; "that's the biggest smallmouth I've ever seen."

"The old me would sell this to Laotians for twenty dollars or more, and that's all the fish would mean to me back then," Embree said, "but now it means so much more: this big girl is headed back in, for Jason."

"For Jason," Luke said.

On the hike back, sopping wet from the waist down, Luke guided Embree along the trail with his phone's flashlight. She stopped, laying into him with a kiss once he approached her, and that's when they saw the first beautiful glimmer: the larval lightning bugs scattered in the leaf litter along the trail's edges, flaring against the night.

"Babe, look!" Embree exclaimed.

"Wow, now that's beautiful, Bubs."

Luke laid into her with another kiss.

"You know I love you, right?" Luke asked.

"Yes, Luke, and I love you, too," Embree whispered.

Luke walked to the side where a bug larvae was blinking and began flipping leaves, looking for it. Embree followed, bending over and taking over the search with her free hands. She flipped a leaf and found a diamond ring, new and twinkling.

"Emb, you're my rock, my love, my searchlight in the dark."

"Oh God," Embree said, growing lightheaded. "You're fucking with me!"

"Emb," Luke paused. "I love you more than anything I've ever loved in this life, and you've brought out of me my better self."

"You're not fucking with me?!"

"Bubs, I love you, and I'll always protect you, even if it costs me my own life; I promise, I will, forever and ever."

Embree nearly fainted, teetering, and Luke lifted the ring.

"My love, you're the greatest thing to ever happen to me. Will you...?"

"Yes, Luke, yes," Embree interrupted drunkenly. "I mean, yes!"

Embree lowered herself by her palms and buckling, shaking knees into the carpet of leaf litter, mud, and acorns, folding in a crab pose and collapsing onto her back and just breathing, with Luke's words echoing about her mind like an artifact ringing one final time—like the Philadelphia freedom bell recommissioned. Now was the time to build and build every which way, a thousand directions to walk at once, starting in that fertile riverbed trail by which the water roiled. Miles off, coydogs howled—

their tumultuous yelping not unlike her own childhood dog, which was freed by bullet from its own metastasizing vertebrae. She clenched fistfuls of leaves, swimming an imaginary backstroke and smiling, knowing that the pain rots souls and love runs red if one lets it, maturing and bracing for the cracking of the bones. Yes, she'd marry— she'd wed the man closest to her heart, finalizing a bond complex like clockwork in the dark. The idea of living out the dichotomy—on one hand, all the achievements and love with Luke, and, on the other hand, suicide in the most excruciating ways, for pain and the precipice of death were old friends—sent shivers through her soul.

God's hand was the soft breeze combing past their skin, the fallen years bygone, and they kissed again, with Luke lying beside her and together already one flesh, savoring it moment by moment—a million micro moments, a million memories, tied together as one.

ACKNOWLEDGMENTS

I would like to thank my family—especially my father, Joe, and my mother, Kelly—for their boundless love and support.

ABOUT ATMOSPHERE PRESS

Atmosphere Press is an independent, full-service publisher for excellent books in all genres and for all audiences. Learn more about what we do at atmospherepress.com.

We encourage you to check out some of Atmosphere's latest releases, which are available at Amazon.com and via order from your local bookstore:

Disruption Games: How to Thrive on Serial Failure, nonfiction by Trond Undheim

Itsuki, a novel by Zach MacDonald

A Surprising Measure of Subliminal Sadness, short stories by Sue Powers

Eyeless Mind, nonfiction by Stephanie Duesing

Saint Lazarus Day, short stories by R. Conrad Speer

My Father's Eyes, a novel by Michael Osborne

The Lower Canyons, a novel by John Manuel

A Blameless Walk, nonfiction by Charles Hopkins

The Horror of 1888, nonfiction by Betty Plombon

Shiftless, a novel by Anthony C. Murphy

White Snake Diary, nonfiction by Jane P. Perry

From Rags to Rags, essays by Ellie Guzman

The Escapist, a novel by Karahn Washington

A Cage Called Freedom, a novel by Paul P.S. Berg

Giving Up the Ghost, essays by Tina Cabrera

Family Legends, Family Lies, nonfiction by Wendy Hoke

Shining in Infinity, a novel by Charles McIntyre

Buildings Without Murders, a novel by Dan Gutstein

ABOUT THE AUTHOR

Tim Galati is an avid novelist and poet, and he is a successful outdoors YouTuber, focusing on fishing, hunting, and foraging in upstate New York. He is also a survivor of severe mental illness, and these outdoor adventures and mental trials often find a way into his writing.